Slave *of*
Conviction

DIARY OF CORRUPTION

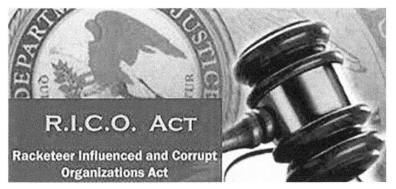

ROY CHAUVIN

Retired LDWF Agent

PAGE PUBLISHING, INC.
Conneaut Lake, PA

First originally published by Page Publishing 2021

ISBN 978-1-6624-3525-6 (pbk)
ISBN 978-1-6624-3526-3 (digital)

Printed in the United States of America

I am dedicating this book to a very dear friend who stood by my side through many of my tribulations. He never swayed during his tough stands, taking up for me even though he was threatened.

"A friend in need is a friend indeed."

Thank you, Gary, for being a part of my life.

Agent Gary Benoit
Died March 1998

INTRODUCTION

After debating almost ten years about resurrecting the atrocities of my career in Louisiana law enforcement, I feel I owe these factual stories to the honest public who live in a vail of fog over the truth about most corruption. Corruption at any level or any degree is just that—corruption. Stories in my book are actual accounts of my day-to-day life as recorded in a daily diary for twenty-seven years. These facts are supported by numerous types of documents, some of which will appear in the book. Most names in the book are fictionalized. However, what's in a name? It is actually the people that are of most importance. Many documents that revealed names were left out so as not to identify, nor embarrass, those who already know who they are as portrayed in the story. A Cajun saying "C'est la vie," or "That's life," will apply and hang a bittersweet hat on their heads. The difference in Louisiana politics is that it's thrown in your face, open for the public to see—brazen, unfettered, and immoral. Fairness and honesty are fictitious terms that burn the mouths of the corrupt when spoken.

I wrestled with the title of the book as well. Should I present the hard facts of a diary of corruption, or should I release my internal struggles to achieve fairness and honesty in a cult that perceived those attributes as a threat? Thus, the title, *Slave of Conviction*. No one wants to be corrupt, but to be honest in a world of politics is a life commitment. One step out of line, and they have you, or own you would be a better term. They will stoop to the lowest of levels to control you. In addition to control, they want secrecy and loyalty. Do what you're told to do at all costs, legal or not.

The price of honesty and justice is very lonely. My strength came from my faith, shaken but never broken. I was perceived as a rogue seeking publicity; however, the unveiling of the truth throughout the media proved to be a saving grace. The media was always looking for a David-and-Goliath story. The media portrayed me as a David on a mission, attacking insurmountable odds. Feeding the media bits and pieces of corruption went on for twenty-seven years. Threatening to expose the truth always kept the tyrant at bay. I always insisted that the media use my name in lieu of the cowardly "according to sources." There was no turning back when I chose this career path.

Even though I was an honor student in a private high school and throughout my four years of college, I was told it was necessary for me to get the endorsement of the local representative. Without this backing, there was no job. The roots of control had begun to sprout. On June 10, 1974, I began my career as a game warden.

CHAPTER 1

Initiation

It did not take long before I was exposed to the corrupt practices of game wardens. At this time, the shrimping season was closed in inside waters in order to allow the shrimp to grow to a larger size. On July 19, 1974, while on a closed-season shrimp patrol in Terrebonne Parish, Louisiana, we approached five large vessels and one smaller boat in the closed area known as Pass Des Isles. As we approached the vessels from the Gulf of Mexico, I noticed we passed by the five larger vessels and went directly to the smaller boat with just the captain aboard. I was told just to observe. Immediately, the captain of the vessel began to complain about the other five vessels we passed who were also shrimping in the closed area. The supervisor, Lieutenant Mooch, said, "Don't worry about them. We have you." As the captain began to derig his equipment for seizure, I noticed he had a half a hand. I could see he struggled at times due to his handicap. In conversation, the captain stated that he got his hand caught in the winch years before.

We seized the nets and shrimp and gave a costly citation to the one-handed fisherman. The other five vessels continued to shrimp in closed waters.

As we passed the first of the five illegal boats on our way out, I asked one agent, "What are we doing? Are we not going to stop the other boats?"

The agent said, "No, these boats belonged to a dealer where the department gets free shrimp."

In addition, I had to watch as Lieutenant Mooch manipulated his dealings with the shrimp dock where we sold the shrimp at the deflated price in order to get his share of shrimp. The agent said, "This is what you signed up for. Get used to it." This was my initiation into corruption. I complained, but I was laughed at and ridiculed.

CHAPTER 2

Uneasy Discretion

Representative Raid

Things went on as usual. I witnessed numerous unmentioned acts of illegal activity by department personnel. Then in the fall of 1976, a series of events defined my path for the rest of my career. There was an unwritten rule that you should not pursue any case involving the federal government and ducks. Those cases were out of the control of the politicians and could not disappear without consequences from the United States Attorney.

On September 19, 1975, I received my first uncomfortable call from a representative asking where the feds were working. I was given the phone number at the representative camp in order to warn him. In September of 1976, an operation was set up with me and a group of federal agents working the top politicians in the state. The hunt was to take place at the representative's camp. Prior to the raid, I was ordered by my supervisors to stay out of the area. In order to prevent selective enforcement, I told the supervisors I would stay out of the area, knowing that a raid was planned. The feds had great concern that I would be fired. I told the feds if I lose my job, then it was not worth having.

On September 18, 1976, the raid went as planned with several citations issued for illegal duck hunting. The feds gathered at my house after the raid. It was shortly thereafter I received a phone call from the state representative. I allowed the feds to listen to the call. The representative belligerently asked if I was with the feds on his place that morning. I told the representative that I was in the area. Expletives abound stating I was told not to go back there. I told the representative, "Yes, but I went anyway."

The berating continued at a blistering pace. The representative stated, "I am hunting with the man, and you should have stayed away."

I asked, "Who was the man?"

He shouted, "The governor, boy. The governor." I said nothing while he continued to verbally assault me. I was not the least bit upset because I knew I was being fair.

Later that day, Captain Ram called asking, "Did you go back on that property? Weren't you ordered not to go back there?"

I told Captain Ram, "Yes."

He stated, "I cannot protect you anymore." I asked Captain Ram what he meant by that remark. Captain stated, "You are on your own with this one. I cannot believe you did that knowing the governor was there. This is bad!"

Immediately, October 2, 1976, the Houma Daily Courier newspaper got wind of the incident and called the chief of enforcement for a comment. The staff did not know how to answer the poignant questions.

Not long after the incident, there was a series of brow-beating meetings with the entire rank of supervisors. My intention at one meeting was to stand firm and hold my ground, even though my ground shrunk to a tiny island. A very unscrupulous ranking official took the lead.

Major Rabbit stated, "Let me get this straight: You were told by your immediate supervisor to stay out of the area. Is that correct?"

I hesitated, smiled, and said, "Yes."

Major Rabbit asked why I was smiling. I told him I would not be intimidated by him, or anyone. Major Rabbit accused me of disobeying a direct order. I responded by saying that I disobeyed an illegal order. Clarifying this statement, I told Major Rabbit that the department did not have the authority to give an illegal order. I asked for the orders in writing so that there would be no misunderstandings to interpret. Major Rabbit began shouting that I was crazy. I asked the major if it was fair to the other people I caught that day. You are not here to protect them. Major Rabbit stated that I would probably lose my job. I told Major Rabbit I would not go down without a fight. Major Rabbit ordered me to apologize to the representative in a face-to-face meeting that he would arrange. I agreed to the meeting, unknowing to them, I had no intention to apologize.

On October 6, 1976, I received a phone call from a very prominent attorney from Houma, Louisiana. Attorney Manipulate stated that he had talked to the governor. During his conversation with the governor, it was revealed that the governor told the representative to "cool it." The conniving attorney offered the governor a place to hunt. October 7, 1976, the governor, according to the Attorney Manipulate, told him that he, the governor, was not going back to hunt with the representative, his close friend, due to the incident. The governor wanted to know if I would go on Attorney Manipulate's duck lease. Attorney Manipulate told the governor, "No." The governor told the representative to call Attorney Manipulate. During this informative call from Attorney Manipulate, I told him that he misled the governor about my whereabouts at any given time. Attorney Manipulate questioned, "I would not come on his place, would I?" I told Attorney Manipulate that I had no reason to go on his place unless I heard that violations were taking place. The attorney arrogantly stated that he could put the governor in a place that I could not get too. I told Attorney Manipulate that now he was challenging me. Attorney Manipulate grudgingly said, "Would you come on my place?" I told Attorney Manipulate not to trust me because he had overstepped his bounds by promising the governor that I would not go on his place. I told Attorney Manipulate to hunt legally, and he and his guests won't have a problem.

The Anti-Apology

On October 28, 1976, as anticipated, a meeting was arranged with the representative. As I walked into his office, I noticed a classmate of mine sitting to the right. There were two guys in suits standing next to this lavish leather chair much like a throne, where the representative sat shouting orders on the phone, telling someone to build that fence twice as tall to keep those f——ing game wardens out. Everyone in the room laughed. The representative ended the conversation and asked me, "What did I want?" I told him I was there to talk as ordered by Major Rabbit. He quipped, "Talk." I told him I wanted to talk in private. He told me not to tell him what to do. I said, "I am leaving." He agreed and sent everybody away.

He started by saying, "What the f——you were thinking coming on my property?" I let the representative rant and rave for twenty minutes about how important he was. As it turned out, the whole purpose of the meeting, other than berating me, was to discover the identity of my informant. He went on to list the names of the important people at his camp that day and how insignificant I was in the scheme of things.

I got tired of his ranting and then threw a question out to him sarcastically, "How many wood ducks did you kill that Saturday morning during the teal-only season?"

He abruptly stood up and asked, "Are you asking me, or are you accusing me of violating?"

I replied, "I am only asking you a question."

The representative called his secretary into his office to take notes. I told him I would not talk with her in the office, and he would never find out who was my informant. This drove him crazy. I went to the door to leave. He stopped me and agreed to my terms. I asked what he would do to the informant. He arrogantly stated, "Let me worry about that."

The representative then stated that I personally caught someone close to him that day on his lease. I confirmed the case, and I told him I caught others as well. Then the representative's true colors were exposed in his epilogue. "I don't give a f——about them. You can catch anyone you want in my district. I want you to leave me alone." I asked the representative if that was fair for him to have that power to tell people to violate the law and overlook violations. I asked what if the public knew of this philosophy. I told him I could not do that.

I told him he would have to get rid of me if he thought he could. Then the most profound and visual characterization happened.

"I am Representative———, worth 3.2 million dollars." As he put wrist to wrist in a crossing manner, he stated, "I am blood with the governor, and you are my f———n———. I will do what I want to you. You can't do anything. I am going to send your ass to Dry Prong, Louisiana."

I responded, "And that's fair." I told Representative Blood Brother (BB) I was not going to give him the name of my informant, nor would I give him a free ride to violate the law. Representative BB charged at me as if to physically hit me. We stared face-to-face.

He went over to a mirror combing his hair, saying, "I just wasted three hours of my time with you."

I sarcastically stated, "Does this mean that you won't support me for a promotion?"

He shouted, "Get out!" having his bodyguards escort me out of his office. I figured I was gone but not without a fight.

As part of their harassment, the department ordered me not to work in representative BB's voting district. I requested the orders in writing, and they said they can't do that. I let the department know that such orders were illegal. On July 14, 1978, as predicted and promised by representative BB, I was sent for the first time out of my district to a place called none other than Dry Prong, Louisiana. I was there to teach hunter safety to seven hundred 4-H students at Camp Grant Walker. I had a great time with the kids, which proved to be a relaxing trip. I had established a reputation that I was going to catch everyone violating. Different versions of the events with representative BB became public. I was ostracized by the department and agents. I worked alone on many patrols. I had to dot my Is and cross my Ts.

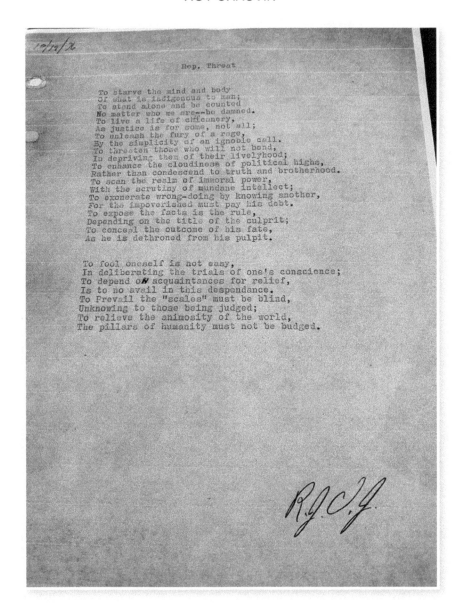

7/12/x

Rep. Threat

To starve the mind and body
Of what is indigenous to man;
To stand alone and be counted
No matter who we are--be damned.
To live a life of chicanery,
As justice is for some, not all;
To unleash the fury of a rage,
By the simplicity of an ignoble call.
To threaten those who will not bend,
In depriving them of their livelyhood;
To enhance the cloudiness of political highs,
Rather than condescend to truth and brotherhood.
To scan the realm of immoral power,
With the scrutiny of mundane intellect;
To exonerate wrong-doing by knowing another,
For the impoverished must pay his debt.
To expose the facts is the rule,
Depending on the title of the culprit;
To conceal the outcome of his fate,
As he is dethroned from his pulpit.

To fool oneself is not easy,
In deliberating the trials of one's conscience;
To depend on acquaintances for relief,
Is to no avail in this despondance.
To Prevail the "scales" must be blind,
Unknowing to those being judged;
To relieve the animosity of the world,
The pillars of humanity must not be budged.

Friends of Blood Brother's Trial

Later that year, I was called into New Orleans Federal Court
to testify in the case of the two close friends of Representative BB.

The attorney for the defendants was a state senator, who had been a US magistrate. The assistant United States attorney met with me stating that he had heard that I was experiencing a great deal of heat in the case, and if I wanted to drop the case, he would protect me. I refused to drop the case, citing the threats. Then in judge's chambers, the case was discussed in front of the senator/defense attorney. The senator stated that I could not win the case because he was a former US magistrate, who knew all the ins and outs. I told the senator if he thought he could win the case, we would not be behind closed doors looking for a deal. Let's go to trial. The assistant United States attorney and judge smiled.

This case was made on the date of The Great Raid. The case centered around a father accompanied by his eleven-year-old son hunting teal ducks. The limit on teal was four teal per person per day. I watched the two individuals hunting. Every time ducks would come into their pond, the father would not let the boy shoot. It was a common practice to shoot someone's limit illegally. As the other agents approached another hunter in the same vicinity, the hunter began shouting, "Game wardens!" The individuals I was watching departed the duck blind by boat and headed in my direction. As they passed my concealed location, the dad in the back of the boat told the young boy to give him a duck.

As the boy watched his dad push the duck under the lilies, he told the boy, as I hid and listened, "Give me another duck."

The boy asked, "What are you doing? Did we do something wrong?"

The dad told the boy to shut up. The boy shook his head in disgust. I marked the spot and let the father-son duo pass my position. They met up with the guy shouting game wardens.

As I approached the group, the first thing out of their mouth was "You know whose lease you are on?" One said, "This is Representative BB's property, and you are not supposed to be back here."

I asked to inspect the father-son duo's limit. The father sarcastically replied, "We have our limit—eight."

I asked the father, "How many ducks did he stuff in the marsh?"

The daddy said, "I didn't get rid of anything." I told the dad that I had observed the entire hunt including the discarding of the over limit. I retrieved the hidden birds and charged the dad.

On the day of the trial, I was sworn in to tell the facts of the case. The assistant United States attorney asked me under oath what the defendants meant when they stated, "You know whose property you're on?" I briefly brought up the threats and history. The defense attorney now had his shot at me. He did not want to talk about the facts in the case but rather inquired about the threat. That proved to be a big mistake by the defense attorney.

Under oath, I detailed the entire ordeal with representative BB. I also implicated the governor. The threats and retaliation were outlined, including but not limited to representative BB's quote stating, "You are my f———n———." The defense attorney objected to try to get me to stop; however, the Assistant United States attorney stated, "You asked, and now he is answering." The judge overruled the objection, and I continued with a barrage of allegations.

There was an attempt to put the eleven-year-old boy on the stand; however, the judge would not allow it. All the defendants were found guilty, and the judge admonished the father and defense attorney's actions.

This trial proved to be a defining moment in my career. I stood up and won. This calculated move by me allowed me to expose the corruption while under oath as a federal witness, which would become my first insurance policy.

On October 21, 1976, I was informed by an anonymous source that the Assistant United States attorney handling the duck case wanted to call for a federal grand jury to investigate witness tampering.

On November 9, 1976, I was informed by federal senior resident agent, Dave Hall, that he went to meet with Representative BB. Representative BB allegedly told Dave Hall that I would not back down from anyone. Dave Hall warned Representative BB that the US Attorney in New Orleans, Louisiana, wanted to call a grand jury over the matter.

On November 10, 1976, allegedly Dave Hall met with Representative BB and the governor.

The public found out, recanting among themselves their own version of events. Some stories were more drastic than the truth but forever making a mark.

Senior resident agent Dave Hall informed me that he had received a call from Congressman Dave Treen, later to be governor of Louisiana, who had been hearing a great deal about the situation. According to Dave Hall, Congressman Dave Treen was asked to intervene but declined. Later that same day, Dave Hall allegedly met with the head of the Louisiana Department of Wildlife and Fisheries. Secretary Snake-Eyes and the chief of enforcement both confirmed that they did not know what to do with me.

CHAPTER 3

The Cult Conspiracy

There were prolific threats made against me. One of the most formidable threats came from other law enforcement officers all the way up the chain of command. Law enforcement officers, in general, with very few exceptions, form a cult. The unwritten word was that you protect your fellow officers at all costs. The cult protected them from unethical, immoral, and illegal practices. Rule number one: Never cite a fellow officer with any type of violation. This was in direct conflict with my philosophy of fairness and honesty. I felt that law enforcement officers should be held to a higher standard than the public. I discovered that the abuse of power was rampant. Many officers felt invincible due to the power of the badge, backed by a gun, and solidified by a loyal cult.

On a patrol in the Lake Theriot area of my parish, I stopped a group of boats for a routine check. Among the people was a detective with the sheriff's office. As I checked everyone, all of whom complied with my check, I came to this detective who flashed his badge in front of everyone in lieu of my request to inspect his fishing license. No one said a word. I asked for his driver's license in order to get information to issue a citation. This seemed trivial to many, but it was to send a message that I was not in their "cult." I had several law-abiding citizens as witnesses. The word spread like wildfire among law enforcement.

In connection with this case was a fishing license citation issued to a high-priced prostitute that was being protected by local law enforcement. I seem to tread on their sacred ground.

On August 26, 1976, I discovered through a high-ranking detective there was talk about getting me for my actions. Early on, I discovered the cult loyalty was defective. Most information came from within the cult from those who feared me, or those who wanted me to get their enemies within the cult.

I underestimated the severity of the threats. I was informed of a meeting at my Louisiana Wildlife and Fisheries Supervisor's Camp. The meeting took place, according to my informant, on August 27, 1976. The meeting/conspiracy allegedly was a venture with my supervisor and a City of Houma detective. The detective allegedly said it was time to do something with Roy Chauvin. On August 28, 1976, at 8 p.m. I received a phone call from a cult member stating that I would be set up at a remote marina, where I was to launch my boat for a night patrol. Obviously, my supervisor, or someone gave the perpetrator my work schedule.

At first, I was apprehensive about the information but then I received another call from the agent I was to work with that night. The agent was very political and could not keep anything to himself. The agent asked if I had received the call from the informant, who we both knew, about the setup. The agent said that a City of Houma detective was going to put cocaine in my left front hubcap on my truck. They would wait down the road and arrest me.

This threat was real with serious consequences. I did not think my adversaries would go that far. I was wrong. I did not trust anyone. I decided to contact the editor of the local newspaper and tell him of the episode. I asked him to say nothing until something happened to me. The editor was very cooperative and agreed.

The plot was foiled, and I heard that the detective was chastised over the plot, and it was my understanding that the detective was livid. He knew that someone in the cult had betrayed him.

Not long after, I was riding in my marked unit in downtown Houma, Louisiana. The same detective, with another person, in their unmarked unit engaged their strobe lights in an attempt to stop me. I had another agent in my car who had reached down, out of sight, to pick up something on the floor of my car. I did not stop, so the detective pulled alongside of me and motioned me to pull over. When the detective saw I was not alone, he turned his strobe light off and sped away. Little did he know that the more he tried to harass me, the stronger I became.

I became more cautious, especially when I worked alone, due to the fact that I was being followed. However, threats continued. On one particular night, I was traveling down a long straight road when a vehicle passed me. The vehicle slowed down almost to a stop in front of me. I began to pass the vehicle, which sped up and stayed in the right lane. I slowed down, and he slowed down. This went on for about one mile. There was a car in the distance in my lane coming head-on with my truck. I made eye contact with the driver, and he smiled. The car was occupied by two other male subjects. It was obvious that the three suspects had an agenda with a specific purpose.

As the car in my lane approached, I decided I had had enough. I rolled down the window of my vehicle on the passenger side, took my .357 magnum service revolver, pointed my gun directly at the driver, and told him I would blow his head off if he did not let me into my lane. I did not have a reputation for this kind of response, which clearly got the driver's attention. The driver slammed on his brakes, and I narrowly avoided a head-on collision. The vehicle continued to follow me for a short distance, then turned off. There was no doubt in my mind that another message was delivered.

I was constantly being informed of threats in an effort to control me. Then one night, at approximately 2 a.m., I was traveling down a rural road heading toward my house. I was in plain clothes in an unmarked vehicle. I had an extremely long day of work. While driving, I noticed two sheriff's units just stopped on the side of the road. I paid no attention. I thought they were just talking to one another. As I passed their location, one deputy pulled out behind me and got very close. There was no traffic, so he had ample opportunity to pass me, but he didn't. The other unit went in the opposite direction. This cat-and-mouse game went on for approximately four miles. I wasn't convinced that he was following me. I came to an intersection

I needed to turn right to go home. Instead, I turned left to determine if he was actually following me. He turned with me staying close. My next move was to enter into a subdivision. I turned left onto a dead-end street. He followed me. At this point, I knew something was wrong. I pulled into a driveway to turn around. The unit passed me and turned into the next driveway. At this point, I decided that I needed to get to a well-lit area in case he stopped me. I turned left again and headed for downtown Houma, Louisiana. The deputy continued to follow me for another five miles mimicking my every move. I headed toward the main intersection in downtown Houma. As I approached the intersection, I noticed two units, one marked and one unmarked, with their lights blaring. The vehicles were facing each other at an angle blocking my passage. Both drivers' doors were open with armed deputies pointing shotguns in my direction. I looked in my rearview mirror, and I noticed two deputies performing the same maneuver with their units—pointing shotguns at me. This was not normal police procedure. This exercise exemplified a felony stop with extreme measures.

One of the deputies behind me began shouting, on his PA system, instructions for me to exit my vehicle with my hands in the air. I had my gun on my side, and I was not going to allow them to see me exit with a gun. I slowly got out of my truck, hands in the air, as a deputy continued to shout orders. The deputy instructed me to face away from him with my hands in the air and head toward the front of my truck. I could hear a deputy approaching from behind as he stated, "Put your hands up and don't move." I did as instructed due to the fact that four guns were aimed in my direction. I asked what the problem was. The deputy stated, "Shut the f——up." The deputy grabbed me and violently threw me up against my truck. He began to pat me down saying nothing, then spun me around with his gun in my face. I explained my badge was in my shirt pocket. He pushed me violently up against the truck again saying, "Shut the f——up! We know who you are."

The deputy then backed away from my truck, all four guns still pointing at me. One by one, they got in their units, turned off the emergency lights, and disappeared in the dark.

The message was very clear. There was a desperate attempt to control me.

In our fairytale lives, we see this at the movies, or on television. Many are fascinated by the fictitious events. However, in reality, these circumstances exist and deliver the harsh message that corruption does exist.

The attempt at control came from politicians, law enforcement, and everyone else who tried to break my will to be fair and honest. I couldn't go to the sheriff and complain. I couldn't go to my department. For the first time, I knew that I was alone. All I had was my faith. I became harder and harder, always looking over my shoulder. This wasn't about Wildlife. It was a struggle for power and control that was out of the corrupt's reach. The culprits became totally frustrated because they could not scare me into submission.

To enhance the severity of these attacks and to add substance and verification to my suspicions, on December 15, 1988, the Lafourche Parish sheriff was the victim of a pipe bomb placed near his car. As it turned out, there was a conspiracy, among four men, to kill the sheriff. All four suspects were either current or former law enforcement officers. The four were allegedly paid $20,000, $8,000 if the bomb only injured the sheriff, and another $12,000 if he was killed. The sheriff kicked a bag containing a pipe bomb placed near his car. The bomb exploded, and the incident nearly severed the sheriff's foot.

One of the four suspects was the detective who tried to set me up to make a stop on my vehicle. As it turned out, the detective was charged in federal court for conspiracy and violation of the Organized Crime Control Act and the illegal possession of a destructive device. The detective entered into a plea agreement and became a government witness in order to avoid the attempted murder charge. For his plea, he was sentenced by a US district judge to spend eleven years in federal prison.

Coincidently, I was chastised by the victim, the sheriff, prior to the bombing, for being too hard on his people. The sheriff told me in a face-to-face meeting that he did not like me and sided with the rest of the politicians. He said I would get mine sooner or later—definite threat. This all began due to the fact that I was stopping eighteen-wheelers to inspect their cargo of alleged seafood. These vehicles were off-loading from large fishing vessels near the Gulf of Mexico. Drugs were a very lucrative business. Highway 1 was the only way out.

After the meeting with the sheriff, I received death threats by phone messages. The same sheriff ran afoul of the law in 1992 while still in office. The sheriff pleaded guilty in federal court to mail fraud, conspiracy, and obstruction of justice. The sheriff spent four years in federal prison. In 1997, he was released from federal prison. The sheriff in Terrebonne Parish during my harassment was allegedly being investigated on 130 counts of criminal activity. He died before he was charged.

At this point in my career, I felt I had survived several shots from the politicians. I became numb to the constant threats and continued the business of law enforcement. My name had become synonymous with fighting corruption. The ongoing feud with Representative BB continued, but I was still around. Politicians began to describe me as crazy. The governor hunted elsewhere as I was told by a source close to the governor that he was uncomfortable with me around.

CHAPTER 4

Who Cares About a Duck?

Ducks Unlimited or Unlimited Ducks

Hunting ducks in South Louisiana was considered a rite of passage. I considered duck hunting a mental disease for some. Even the most intelligent of people somehow forgot how to count. Duck hunting was, and is, a rich man's sport. Many of whom thought they were above the law. This is why the Department of Wildlife and Fisheries had an unwritten rule not to work ducks, much less work with the feds. The temptation to resist killing over the limit of ducks was an insurmountable one that most of the population could not resist. The millions of dollars donated to the local chapters of Ducks Unlimited seemed to be a free ticket to kill as many ducks that they wanted. Different cases come to mind dealing with Ducks Unlimited officials in my area. Two were presidents of local chapters, while another served on the national board of the Ducks Unlimited organization.

The first case involved someone who I thought would never violate. He was president of a bank and had a great deal of respect in the community. Early one morning, during the duck season, I paddled my pirogue, a small boat similar to a canoe, into the marsh before daylight. I concealed my whereabouts and set up surveillance. There was a single hunter in a duck blind overlooking a small pond. Ducks were numerous. The subject appeared to have killed his limit. I watched the subject pick up several ducks while heading in my

24

direction. He came within twenty yards of me, picked up a single duck, then threw the duck in the marsh. I continued to observe as a subject slowly grabbed his gun in a suspicious manner. I decided to reveal my position. The subject grabbed his chest, taking a deep breath, saying, "I thought you were a deer laying in the marsh." He said, "I almost shot you!"

I made a check of his limit asking why he threw that duck away.

He said, "You saw me?"

I said, "Yes."

He put his head down in disgust and shame. I lost sight of the bird due to my concealment. I began an unsuccessful search for the duck. I could not find the bird; therefore, I had no charge. The subject said, "Charge me if you have to. I was wrong and was ashamed." Had I found the bird, I would have charged him; however, due to his sincere reaction, I would not have felt like I accomplished anything. He tried and convicted himself by his emotions.

The next case was one that had different results. After flying over an area, we noticed a very large concentration of ducks in front of two duck blinds. This is usually an indication of bait, which is illegal. Baiting ducks with rice, corn, milo, or any other grain, or substance was a federal violation. Baiting, as we refer to it, was a major problem in south Louisiana. 99 percent of baiting cases were associated with over limit, many of which were extremely over the limit. We went two days before the hunt late one night to retrieve a bait sample in front of the two blinds. The bait sample was good for prosecution evidence for ten days, or until the last grain was gone for ten days.

At first light, shooting began coming from both blinds. We observed numerous ducks being killed. There was an old man hunting alone to my right. He had ducks flying all over him, but he chose to shoot only mallards. The hunter further back shot at everything in range. As the hunt ended, the old man was standing in his pirogue, moving along by a method known as push polling. As he got closer to me, I stood up and identified myself. The first words out of his mouth were, "Chauvin, you got me." The old man was very cooperative and told of the years of abuse and thousands of ducks he had killed. He smiled saying, "I guess it's my time to get caught. No hard feelings, Chauvin." As he shook my hand, I could see by the pile of ducks in his pirogue. He was grossly over the limit. He never denied the bait either.

The son-in-law of the old man was in the farthest blind. He lagged back with a disgusted look on his face. He was charged with hunting over bait, exceeding the legal limit, and not possessing a federal duck stamp. He made a spectacle of himself as he moaned, groaned, and pleaded for mercy and even cried. I recognized him as being the president of the local Ducks Unlimited chapter. He stated that he did not want any publicity. He said it would be very embarrassing to be exposed. The duck stamp was a benchmark of Ducks Unlimited. Not having one should be embarrassing. Somehow, the story made the front page of the local newspaper, and his embarrassment escalated. The old man told his son-in-law he was embarrassing him by his reaction and told him, "Take your medicine." The old man pointed out the fact that we can see Representative BB's camp, and he found it strange that Representative BB was not hunting on opening day. Later, I discovered that one of my ambitious agents who worked with me had warned Representative BB that we were working in his area.

Another case comes to mind involving a multimillionaire who owns thousands of acres of paradise. A man of these means employed many people, and it is hard to keep them all happy. In the infancy of our investigation, we tried to get a key to a critical entrance gate; however, we were denied by the landowner. The false security of that gate provided a perceived barrier, so the owner thought.

A federal agent developed information on the owner from a disgruntled employee, who gave specific details on the blind locations and the system used in order to avoid being caught. It was a common practice for these big-shot landowners to invite numerous people to hunt, telling them not to kill over the limit. We eventually received the key to that critical gate. With that being said, early one morning, federal agent Bill Mellor and I set up surveillance on the landowner and his guests. We documented the killing of several ducks, and, as on cue, the owner exited the blind with his Labrador retriever picking up several ducks, placing them in a sack. The owner headed in our direction with his dog and sack of ducks, leaving his friend in the blind. Our cultivated information was that the landowner would wait for the rest of the hunting party, and he would give his over limit to those who had not killed. We scrambled to hide better for he was coming straight in our direction. I worried about the dog catching us. The landowner came within twenty feet of me. The dog came within five feet; however the landowner was concentrating on his effort to hide the sack of ducks. The landowner went back to the blind and began shooting more ducks. We crawled to the stack of ducks and counted them. In order to distinguish the rest of the ducks from the ducks in the sack, we marked the ducks by clipping the right hind toe of every duck in the sack. We placed the sack of ducks where it had been hidden and backed off. The landowner and his guests continued to hunt, killing many ducks, all of which exceeded the limit.

The other hunters began their trek out of the marsh. The landowner and friend began to pick up their ducks. Upon completion, the landowner and friend retrieved the sack of marked ducks. Just as our informant indicated, several hunters waited for the landowner. We were able to document taking the birds out of the sack by the owner separating the ducks. The entourage came in our direction with the landowner in the lead. We stopped the landowner, who was very cordial. We began inspecting duck limits of the whole party, and to no surprise, everyone was within their limits. Light talk continued until we asked to take custody of all the ducks. We gathered up all the birds, separating the marked birds from the rest. The marked birds were scattered throughout the hunting party's limits. The landowner asked what was going on.

I told the landowner, "I could have kissed you on the cheek. You were so close to me when you picked up that sack of ducks."

The landowner stated, "You can't prove your case."

At this time, we showed the landowner the marked birds. He put his head down in disgust. The landowner was formerly on the national board of trustees of Ducks Unlimited. The owner pleaded guilty in federal court and allegedly paid a $10,000 fine, nothing more than a slap on the wrist. The landowner was quoted in the Saint Paul Pioneer Press in a nationwide article entitled *Empty Skies: Ducks in Crisis*. This quote states:

> I wasn't one of the big duck killers in Louisiana, but I'll admit I never stopped at a limit from the time I was first taken hunting as a kid until I was caught. Nor did anyone I know.

This special report created quite a stir in Louisiana. The Louisiana Wildlife and Fisheries denounced its findings. I was condemned for my comments; however, I received numerous letters of support from throughout the Midwestern states. Once again, the word spread like wildfire that I was catching everyone.

Federal Fix

The brief time I was in law school, I was told that 90 percent of all cases would be settled behind closed doors. Many times, the truth would never expose the client to criticism. How true that was. I always had trust in the feds. The secrecy and judicial system were untouched by corruption. So I thought. In November of 1977, a series of events took place that crushed my faith in the federal system. I was being recruited for a federal agent position at the time. I was apprehensive about leaving an area that I was nowhere close to fixing. I discovered that my presence had an impact on preserving and protecting wildlife. During this time, we spent a great deal of time flying looking for bait. While flying over an area, we discovered a large yellow streak in front of a blind with hundreds of feeding ducks. We knew it was corn we were observing. The next day, we went to the location and took a sample of the corn. The quantity and placement of the bait indicated a certain arrogance. There was no attempt to conceal the bait, and corn was one of the easiest grains to detect. Through the windows of the camp, we noticed approximately one hundred sacks of corn.

On November 5, 1977, a federal agent and I set up surveillance on the baited pond. There were three men and one woman hunting. All four subjects shot several birds and headed in our direction. Upon checking, I recognized one individual as an attorney. The attorney pleaded with me for some sort of leniency; however, his efforts were insincere and somewhat arrogant. The other man was a successful real estate developer. The woman presented as an immediate problem for them. The attorney pleaded with me not to give the woman a citation. All four were cited and released. Cut-and-dry case, I thought.

On November 7, 1977, I received a call from Captain Flip and Flop who wanted details of the case as per request from Secretary Snake-Eyes of the Louisiana Department of Wildlife and Fisheries. For unknown reasons, the attorney allegedly told Secretary Snake-Eyes that I was after Representative BB. This was only to cloud the issue. These allegations reared an ugly head once again.

On February 2, 1978, the trial began in federal court with US Magistrate Egret. I could see that the defense attorney had a copy of my case report, which he received outside the normal procedure. I asked where he got my report. He stated, "I have friends in Baton Rouge [Louisiana, the capital] and especially in your department." This set the tone for the case—backdoor corruption and politics. The case was solid, and the defendants were found guilty before US Magistrate Egret.

The defense attorney vowed to appeal. On May 22, 1978, the assistant United States attorney in charge of the case stated that in his effort to answer the appeal, he listened to the tapes of the trial. The assistant United States attorney stated he went for a second time to listen to the tapes, but they had been destroyed. This incident was grounds to grant the appeal. On July 5, 1978, a new trial was granted by a US district judge on the grounds that the trial tapes were inaudible. A US marshal outside the courtroom stated that all one had to do was to place a magnet across the tapes, and they would be destroyed. True or not, the tapes were suspiciously destroyed. The case was sent back to the US Magistrate Egret for the second trial. I figured we had no problem because this same judge found the defendants guilty in the first trial, and the facts would be the same.

On July 21, 1978, the second trial took place. As I walked into the courtroom, I saw the defendant/attorney up on the bench with his hand on the shoulder of the magistrate looking at pictures. The defendant/attorney looked at me and smiled sarcastically. I had a bad feeling that the fix was on. We went to trial presenting the same evidence as in the first trial when they were found guilty. There was a lack of cross-examination from the defendant's attorney. I said to myself, "I got them." To my astonishment US Magistrate Egret stated, "Not guilty on all counts." The magistrate said his decision was based on his belief that the defendant had placed the corn out after the hunt; therefore, the defendant did not hunt over the bait. I ran outside into the hall very visibly upset. My federal agent friend said, "We had been duped, and there was nothing you can do."

I had another trial that day with an old man with four coots over the limit. The old man could not read or write. I remember him signing the citation with an X. He was outside the courtroom wearing a torn shirt, when he asked me to help him. The old man said, "All I like to do is hunt. I don't have many years left. I'm going to plead guilty. I don't want to lose my hunting rights." The marshals called the old man into court, and I followed. I shouted to the assistant United States attorney that I wanted the case against the old man to be dismissed. I stormed out of the courtroom in protest. Two US marshals came to get me to testify. I told the marshals to tell the judge that I refuse to testify. The marshals were going to force me into the courtroom. I told them that I will resist, and you'll have to put me in jail. I stated, "While I am in jail, I will call the media to interview me behind bars. Go tell the magistrate." The marshal said, "The magistrate will hold you in contempt." I stayed in the hall. The old man was tried without my testimony and was found guilty. The magistrate took away his hunting rights. The old man came out of the courtroom dejected and sincerely thanked me for my help.

Those circumstances compounded my resentment. I stormed back into the courtroom unafraid because everyone knew that justice had been compromised. As I walked into the courtroom, on a mission, the magistrate was still on the bench. There was the assistant United States attorney, a US fish and wildlife agent, and two US marshals in the courtroom. I shouted at the judge, asking him how he could do that—find them guilty and then not guilty. The judge did not answer. The US marshals tried to quiet me stating, "The judge will hold you in contempt." I continued by saying, "I had a lot of respect for your position"—speaking to the judge—"but no more." What happened today was rotten. The judge stood up and ordered me into his chambers alone. The judge said, "I know you are upset, and I don't blame you, but the truth of the matter is that I had no choice." The judge said, "I am nearly seventy years old, and I want to retire within the next two years." The judge said he had to change the verdict due to pressure from one of the US district judges. He stated that he was due to be reappointed by the US district judges, and he was told to take care of the case. I told the judge that his actions were an excuse to rationalize a reason. "You prostituted yourself for personal gain." The judge said nothing for a minute. Then he said that I had a rotten job. He asked me to go back to law school, and he would hire me as his law clerk. I turned his job down as well as the federal agent's job.

Captain Ram, who happened to be a defense witness as custodian of records, stated, "I told you those feds would screw you."

Later that month, the initial charges were made public in the front page of the local newspaper. All the names were published. A couple of days later, the defendant/attorney who spearheaded the corruption called me. The attorney said it was dirty for me to leak that story to the press. He stated that the story had created a great deal of personal trouble for all concerned. I did not confirm leaking the story, but I told him that is what you get for playing dirty politics.

I wonder who it was that leaked the story. *Ha! Ha! Ha!*

CHAPTER 5

The Crash

It was public knowledge that I did not get along with the politicians, nor my department. I continued to work in spite of a certain element of the public, who seemed to have free shots at me. The department, at times, would look for minute technicalities in cases in order to discipline me. I noticed an increase in the outlaw public that threatened me openly. There were physical threats as well as the old-school game of threats to get my job through the politicians. I almost became immune to those threats due to my survival rates.

This brewing lack of respect reared an ugly head on the night patrol of November 23, 1979. I had a very small boat with a very large motor. My boat was considered a chase boat. In retrospect, the boat was very unsafe, probably why I got it in the first place. That night, we were working night hunting of deer, which was a high priority. The penalty for hunting deer at night carried a mandatory thirty days in jail and forfeiture of all equipment seized.

The judges often complained that murder carried a zero-to-life sentence, but kill a deer, and the sentence starts at thirty days in jail. This patrol started out with four agents and two boats. Two agents complained about the patrol and headed to the district attorney's camp. It was a very cool night with a light fog hovering over the water. The agent with me was new and did not know the area. South Louisiana is a maze of canals and lakes.

While traveling without lights for concealment, a dangerous tactic, I observed a light to my right that appeared to be night hunting. Upon investigation, we discovered that the subjects were indeed night hunting. They would shine their light on the banks of the canal and would turn around to come out in the dark. I decided that we would hide and let them pass us in the dark. I positioned my boat behind the suspects' boat while running approximately thirty-five miles per hour. I could see there were three subjects standing behind the windshield. I instructed the new agent to get ready as I turned on my spotlight and identified ourselves. The boat sped up. I began nudging the suspects' boat by pushing on his motor at high speeds. The subjects would not stop. We were traveling in a tree-lined canal where trees hung over the water. The light fog made it difficult to see. I kept the light on the three subjects who began to hit low-lying tree limbs. They still did not stop. I instructed the agent to get his sawed-off shotgun ready. The chase went on for approximately ten minutes. This was very dangerous; therefore, I instructed the young agent to shoot the suspects' motor as I pulled alongside. We came to a T in the canal, where I lost sight of the subjects in the fog. Thinking the suspects had gone straight and crashed, I jumped a wave to position myself on the right side of the boat in case they did not crash. The subject's boat came out of the fog at a collision angle with me. They pushed me to the right side of the canal. Water was flying everywhere. We began bumping into the subjects' boat, which was much larger than my boat. I was against the subjects' boat, two feet from the motor. The subjects' boat continued to push me into the trees. I told the agent to "take the gun off safety, and when I tell you, shoot the motor."

I never had the opportunity to tell the agent to shoot. Everything went blank. At this point, I did not know what happened. I felt myself hanging halfway out of the boat with my hands in the water. I could not move. I heard the young agent talking to the other two agents who were miles away. The young agent said, "I don't know where we are." The agent in the other boat asked if we were all right. The young agent said, "No, I think Roy is dead." I still could not move, or talk. I could hear the conversation. The agent pulled me into the boat, and I gradually became conscious. The young agent was very nervous, as he held a towel on the top of my head. The agent said that I had a very bad head wound that needed attention now. I left my wrecked boat in the marsh, and the other two agents brought me to a hospital thirty miles away. As a result of the crash, I received thirty stitches in the top of my head, and an X-ray revealed that I had a possible vertebrae fracture.

No one called me the next day from my department. Instead, the following day, the department called to inform me that the state did not have insurance on any boat powered over fifty horsepower. My boat had a 150 horsepower motor. I was ordered to park my boat. No investigation was ever done. The word spread among the outlaws, and a mirage of violators began to take credit. The impact of the crash was so violent the short windshield, which reached to the middle of my chest, the steering wheel, which was lower, and the motor cover were shattered off. Once again, I felt like I was protected by divine intervention.

CHAPTER 6

New Governor and Promotion

On January 1, 1980, we had a new governor, Dave Treen, and a new secretary of Louisiana Department of Wildlife and Fisheries, Jesse Guidry. The old cronies within the department now had a new boss. Immediately things began to take shape for the better. I was called into the new secretary's office alone. I was apprehensive, but I was told by Secretary Guidry that there would be absolutely no pressure placed on me while doing my job. Secretary Guidry said, "All we want you to do is enforce the law, and we will back you." Finally, music to my ears!

To test my loyalty to the administration, I had a clandestine meeting with two local state representatives and a confidant of the new governor. The meeting took place at a legislative cookout in Baton Rouge, Louisiana, on June 18, 1980. My nemesis, Representative BB, was now a more-powerful senator. Senator BB voiced his displeasure with the new administration. The three asked me to work on Senator BB. They said anything I did would have to be secret due to a leak on the fourth floor of the capital. I would have clearance and backing of the governor.

There was a reorganization of the enforcement division. I sought a newly created position, captain of District 9B on February 5, 1981. I spoke to Secretary Guidry about my quest. The secretary said the governor wanted politics out of decision-making and wanted the position to be competitive. Due to my lack of politics, the position became a hot potato, tossed back and forth. Months went by, and the only position statewide that had not been filled was captain of District 9B.

On April 24, 1981, I was informed that the editor of the Houma Daily Courier newspaper told the district attorney that an influential attorney had requested the feds to investigate the district attorney. My relationship with the district attorney began to deteriorate due to the fact that he supported one of my rivals for the new position. I would not honor his request to back off the promotion. In spite of the day-to-day rumblings concerning the promotion, I still had to go to work to answer complaints from the public. I had laid the groundwork and support for the promotion. It was time to let it go.

Internal Affairs Investigation

In April, I began an investigation into the illegal harvesting of oysters. I called one agent for help. The agent said he couldn't help because the lieutenant had him doing construction at the district attorney's camp. On April 30, 1981, I served the warrants without help. The agent asked me to help him get out of the camp building patrols. During the time that District 9B had no supervisor, Major Boots, from Baton Rouge, took over during this crisis. On May 1, 1981, I asked Major Boots for help in the oyster investigation. The major wanted to know where the other agents were. I told the major that two agents were working at the district attorney's camp. The major ordered me to write a statement of the details. I refused, at first, citing the potential problems. The major then ordered me to write the statement, especially outlining the reason why I had no help on patrols. On May 13, 1981, not to my surprise, Colonel Ram called me to ask if I had given my statement to a representative—should have been a rhetorical question. I said, "No." The colonel stated someone stole a copy of the report from Major Boots's desk. Here we go round and round.

On May 15, 1981, my lieutenant, who worked at the district attorney's camp, called me stating that the district attorney, two representatives, and Senator BB were meeting with Secretary Guidry on

May 18, 1981. The call by the lieutenant was to intimidate me. The two representatives were the same ones who conspired on June 18, 1980, with me to get Senator BB.

On May 16, 1981, Major Boots called to say Secretary Guidry ordered him to bring the reports to the State Crime Lab in an effort to find evidence as to who stole the report. The major stated, "Remember, I ordered you to write the report." The disgruntled group and turncoats already had a preconceived attitude about me. So what's the use in blaming the major?

District Attorney Threat

The meeting went as planned on May 18, 1981, with the secretary and politicians. Later that afternoon, the district attorney called me into his office. He threw my report at me across the table and said, "I am going to be on your ass like gravy on rice." He stated that I should have never written that report. He stated he would do his best to put me in jail. He said that I knew of the agreement with the former Secretary Snake-Eyes and Governor Rico that the camp would be used as a base of operations. This agreement solidified his written lease with the Land Company.

I told the district attorney that the old administration was no longer in power, and the new administration had granted me a shot to make things fair and honest. The district attorney said that in three years, the old administration would regain power, and he would be appointed secretary of the Louisiana Department of Wildlife and Fisheries. I asked if he would send me to Dry Prong. He sarcastically laughed saying he would use his office to be on me constantly. After this, I marked him off the list of supporters.

On June 24, 1981, I was instructed to meet with internal affairs to discuss another event in the misuse of state equipment by the same lieutenant and another agent. This investigation centered around my observation on November 9, 1980. The internal affairs officer stated that the lieutenant had already admitted wrongdoing by carrying lumber in his state boat to his camp. I told internal affairs that I arrived at a very busy boat landing after a 3:00 a.m. duck patrol.

Upon arrival, I saw the lieutenant launching his personal boat with his state truck. Also, the agent with the lieutenant was launching the state boat, full of lumber, with his state truck. Neither agents were wearing uniforms. The one agent in the boat loaded with lumber decided to write a citation to cover his ass, especially after he saw us arrive. The problem was that he did not have a ticket book, negating his intentions to work. He borrowed my ticket book to write a registration violation. The person he wrote the citation to asked me if he could haul lumber to the lieutenant's camp in the state boat. I told him no, but we live in Louisiana. The interview terminated, and I heard nothing more.

On June 25, 1981, Major Boots informed me that the secretary's appointment was not yet confirmed by the Senate due to Senator BB's stand. Senator BB was also holding up the entire state budget due to the governor's threat to promote me.

At the beginning of the struggle to become captain of District 9B, I wrote and hand-delivered my resume to ten influential people whom I knew supported me. It became power versus power. Everyone's ego got involved, which was good for me. Friendships were tattered and torn. Threats ran amok as my people worked the politicians.

Promotion Conflict

On June 23, 1981, one of Governor Treen's appointees to the Louisiana Department of Wildlife and Fisheries Commission allegedly threatened the governor. The commission member stated he would resign if I received the promotion. According to sources, I guess the governor had enough and told the commissioner to resign. The governor stated he was backing me for the promotion. Daily, I was informed of high-level meetings with heated discussions. Everyone seemed to have an opinion. On July 23, 1981, I was informed that, allegedly, the wife of the AFLCIO president and the wife of the governor had thrown their support behind me. There was a circus of stars that defined the political arena, which existed in Louisiana. How could the state function by dealing with such trivial matters? Do you think that anyone was thinking about wildlife during this debacle? Most certainly not. What a shame.

On June 24, 1981, I was instructed by Secretary Guidry to give a more detailed affidavit to internal affairs about infractions by my lieutenant. This lieutenant received his promotion by employing these tactics and favors for politicians.

On June 29, 1981, I was informed that the superpowers of lower Lafourche Parish were to meet. A powerful shipyard owner was to be the mediator to quell the storm of events created by the commission member of Louisiana Department of Wildlife and Fisheries who was also present. Two of my influential supporters were there to defend me. After the meeting, I was informed that the Louisiana Department of Wildlife and Fisheries commission member allegedly met with the governor to resign. The governor, upset, said he was appointing me captain, according to sources.

The qualifications for taking the civil service exam for the position was supposed to expire on July 28, 1981; however, that date, for some political reason, was extended to August 10, 1981.

Finally, on August 14, 1981, I was appointed captain of District 9B by the governor. The secretary said the only condition was that I make some sort of effort to get along with the politicians, but under no circumstances was I to compromise my stance of honesty and justice. Wow! Music to my ears. Most suitable was the quote by Dr. Martin Luther King, "Free at last. Free at last. Free at last." However, in my case, the freedom didn't last.

Agents began to retaliate immediately. They would not show up for work, calling in sick and even quitting. I knew there was a great deal of resentment, and this was a knee-jerk reaction to my appointment. I just had to give them time.

On September 24, 1981, at his request, I met with a city councilman who is in the political loop. This was the same councilman who warned me about the detective and drug set up. The councilman stated that a group of politicians from the area had met with the former governor. The gist of the meeting amounted to a conspiracy about my future with the Louisiana Department of Wildlife and Fisheries. It was my understanding that the former governor allegedly told the group to leave me alone or someone would go to jail. One blowfish politician stated he was going to do his best to see that I went to jail.

To retaliate, the district attorney in Terrebonne Parish began to scrutinize every case with a prejudice microscope, finding fault in similar cases he had prosecuted before my appointment.

Most of our cases were misdemeanors, so I spoke to the city judge, who had jurisdiction over the cases, to take over the charges. We set up a system where the charges were filed directly with city court. Later, a bill in the Louisiana state legislature gave city court parish-wide jurisdiction. This was done due to the district attorney's retaliation against me. This move infuriated the district attorney.

I was content to be out of the loop of clandestine meetings, cover-ups, attacks, and defending myself. However, there were a great deal of things going on that I was not aware.

On April 27, 1982, I was ordered to Baton Rouge headquarters to meet again with internal affairs of the Department of Wildlife and Fisheries and a state police captain in charge of the State Police Internal Affairs. I was told to bring documentation on misuse of state equipment by my lieutenant and dates of threats made by the district attorney of Terrebonne Parish.

On April 28, 1982, I met with both internal affairs divisions; however, this seemed to be a more serious interview. I was told off the record that a request was made to begin an organized crime investigation into threats made by the district attorney of Terrebonne Parish. The state police captain placed me under oath and said the interview would be recorded and transcribed to a signed notarized affidavit. In my statement, I detailed the same threats the district attorney had made earlier for exposing the misuse of state equipment at his personal camp. The agent who worked at the camp gave a statement.

I began to meet and speak to numerous civic and sportsman's organizations. Invariably, the topic of discussion drifted into politics. I was asked direct questions; therefore, I gave direct answers at the astonishment of those attending. I was often asked why I fought so hard and did not give up. My answers usually follow the same format. The animals and wildlife I am supposed to care for are all but forgotten in the skirmish. I told them that I protected their peaceful times away from the office fishing and hunting, their break from the hassles of everyday life. This was as much a part of my job as anything else.

I was also asked what motivated me. I relayed a story about a late-afternoon patrol on a slick calm day with the sun setting on a large lake, where I observed a man, alone in his boat in the middle of all this water, casting a rod and reel. The man did not catch a fish but continued to cast this tiny bait in this broad expanse of water in the expectation of what. I asked myself, "What was he thinking as his efforts continued? Was he at peace in this beautiful Sportsman's Paradise?" Then I asked myself what my role was in the natural scheme of things. A mellow calm engulfed my body, and I knew that I was on the right track. The fisherman never knew I was there, nor did he know how his actions inspired me to continue the fight. This break from reality was often needed, but good things seem to fade away faster than the serenity they bring.

On June 8, 1982, the district attorney, in a move to validate his threats, had spearheaded a case involving the agent who worked at his camp and gave a signed affidavit, outlining his violations, to both state police and Louisiana Department of Wildlife and Fisheries internal affairs. The agent was placed in jail, but the case was immediately overturned by the appeals court in Louisiana.

Obviously, things were on another roller coaster in Baton Rouge headquarters. On June 11, 1982, I was called in to Baton Rouge to meet with Secretary Guidry, the organized crime task force of the Louisiana State Police and the Louisiana Attorney General's office. The meeting centered around serious threats made against me by unrevealed sources. I was told to take extra precautions on my day-to-day patrols. Now there was a criminal element in the mix, and the secrecy of the meeting alarmed me. All I could think about was the assassination attempt with the pipe bomb and the city detective's involvement.

On August 22, 1982, at the Louisiana Agents' Association Convention in Many, Louisiana. The secretary presented me with the agent of the year award. The award had many implications, but the main reason for the award was a show of support by the administration.

Soon thereafter, I was asked by Major Silver Tongue to do a live radio show in New Orleans, Louisiana. The Mary Foster Program was a popular live radio show that allowed the public to discuss controversial issues concerning the Louisiana Department of Wildlife and Fisheries. This radio show exposed me to a wider base of people.

CHAPTER 7

The Showdown

Gill Net Gumbo

On April 26, 1983, I was called by a local radio station KMRC in Morgan City, Louisiana, and asked to do a live radio show on what was going on in Terrebonne Parish between the Louisiana Department of Wildlife and Fisheries' agents and the district attorney. Well, I had had enough threats; therefore, I unloaded on all the corruption.

On April 27, 1983, I received a call from a TV reporter in New Orleans, Louisiana. The reporter wanted me to accompany him to the district attorney's camp, where he was to interview the district attorney. I told the reporter that I could not go due to the threats. The reporter flew to the district attorney's camp and interviewed him. Upon returning, the reporter told me he was glad I did not go because the district attorney was very belligerent and threatening. There was a short piece aired about the problems.

On May 19, 1983, Colonel Ram called me to say that I was wrong for going to the media. I had crossed the line with Colonel Ram, but I had the backing of Secretary Guidry. The colonel was playing both sides of the political fence, a tactic in which I often became the scapegoat. The colonel secretly sided with anti-administration old cronies. This was done to feather his nest in case of a change in administration in two years.

On July 6, 1983, Colonel Ram had me meet him in the field. He was very upset with me. He stated that he wanted to handle things. I told Colonel Ram that he was not very successful in the past, stating such things as "I cannot protect you anymore. You are on your own." I told him that he wanted me to stop fighting for my cause, as it was called, when I finally had a little breathing room. The colonel left me with the threat, "Every dog has his day." I responded by saying that the bite doesn't hurt if the dog has no teeth. That wasn't taken well by the colonel who had thrown me to toothy dogs before.

On July 9, 1983, in order to flex his muscles, Colonel Ram sent me on a patrol set up by my nemesis district attorney to please a woman seafood dealer over a gill net complaint. This act was very significant for future development.

Reflections

The district attorney was quoted as saying, "Roy Chauvin is incompetent, incapable of leading men, and unqualified to be in his current job. It's not going to get any better [in Terrebonne] until they put Chauvin someplace else." When the district attorney was confronted by Bob Marshall, outdoor editor of the Times-Picayune Newspaper, about my statement concerning agents working at his camp, the district attorney exclaimed, "I told Chauvin, 'F——you, and the horse you rode in upon.'" The district attorney stated, "He took a cheap shot at me."

This article exemplified the arrogance of a man who thought he was invincible, much like King Richard the Third—a horse. A horse. My kingdom for a horse. His bitterness toward me would eventually lead to his downfall. His rants also made me stronger in the eyes of the public on a statewide level. My struggle for fairness and honesty was indeed taking shape.

CHAPTER 8

Crooked Game Wardens

Corruption Revealed

On July 26, 1983, a lone agent drove to my house, crying as he exited his vehicle. He said, "I can't take it anymore. My conscience is killing me." I asked the distraught agent what was wrong. He began telling his story, which eventually wound up on the front page of the Houma Daily Courier newspaper on September 25, 1983.

In this revelation on July 26, 1983, the agent said that he and three other agents in Lafourche Parish would shrimp in close season, seize shrimp, and steal the shrimp. They falsified reports and sometimes sold illegally taken shrimp for financial gain.

The agent outlined for the reporter the dates of July 20 through July 24, 1983. The newspaper story recants my investigation during this time period.

The only thing missing from the report was that on July 24, 1983, the agent said he couldn't participate anymore. This was a threat to the other three agents. The three agents placed the informant on a barge in the middle of the night in an effort to intimidate him. Later that night, the three agents returned to the barge with their boats full of illegal gains. The three, at one point, terrorized the agent/informant, holding a gun to his head. That was when the agent came to me. The four agents were immediately suspended, and an investigation began. I was ordered by staff attorneys and Secretary Guidry not to speak to the press.

The informant's revelation after months of investigation turned out to be truthful with physical evidence to back up his claims. In an attempt to discredit me, former agent G, who resigned under investigation for misuse of state equipment at the district attorney's camp, took shots at me in a September 22, 1983, article in the Houma Daily Courier newspaper. Agent G stated that it was a common practice for agents to take seafood. On September 23, 1983, Agent G aired his complaint that I was hired to get rid of him and the other four agents that resigned. These antics were sorted out in the Daily Comet newspaper in Thibodaux, Louisiana.

The four agents admitted to very serious wrongdoing, and there was substantial evidence to ensure their convictions on numerous felony counts. One may wonder why the agents weren't charged with their crimes. Why were they able to resign? The reason why no charges were filed was due to the fact that the agents were right in one claim. It was a common practice to take illegal shrimp. I had to watch it go on for years; my complaints fell by the wayside. I was told by supervisors not to rock the boat, or you will fall out.

One of the accused agents boldly stated, "They can't charge me. If they do, I will rat on everybody in Baton Rouge headquarters that got some of the shrimp, frogs, fish, ducks, deer, and anything else I would seize." This cover-up blackened the soul of the department for years. When the department had a chance to fix it, they blew it.

While Agent G defended his friends who resigned in the newspaper articles, he failed to mention that one of these agents had been under state and federal investigation.

If I may digress, this story began on November 18, 1976, when I attended a meeting in the New Orleans's Federal Courthouse. At this meeting, I overheard the sheriff of Terrebonne Parish was under investigation. The sheriff went after anyone he thought was after him. At one point, the sheriff blamed the district attorney. Sometime later, the district attorney, who I was friends with at the time, called Agent G and I to immediately go to his camp and get all the National Guard Armory equipment out of the camp. Not knowing the reason, we complied. He wanted the equipment at his house as soon as possible. Upon arrival, it became known that the old sheriff had been conducting an investigation into a recent theft at the National Guard Armory in Terrebonne Parish. As part of the investigation, the old sheriff secured a search warrant for the district attorney's camp. Someone let the cat out of the bag and allegedly warned the district attorney. The warrant was squashed when the district attorney allegedly turned over the sought-after evidence. It was my understanding that the old sheriff was allegedly facing 130 counts of wrongdoing. The old sheriff died before the case was resolved.

The kicker and relevance to this story was that on occasion the district attorney would set up patrols with the Louisiana State Police narcotics agents to assist me. Their aggressive demeanor was not suited for wildlife law enforcement. I did not like working with them. As it turned out, my intuition was correct. The chief suspects in this theft ring were the state police narcotics officers and one Wildlife agent. As with any state investigation of this magnitude, rumors of cover-ups ran rampant. This wildlife agent was suspended during this investigation. As a result of the lengthy investigation, one of the narcotics officers either pleaded guilty or was found guilty. This narcotic officer spent several years in prison for these crimes. The wildlife agent came back to work and was never charged.

While on suspension, the agent was the subject of another investigation involving the shooting of ducks illegally. In spite of my orders not to work ducks, the department would routinely send me to solve their problems due to my work ethic. I worked for wildlife and not to carry out vendettas for politicians. I was always skeptical of these assignments and on constant guard of a setup. The informant in this case was a state representative and, later, a US congressman. It seems as though the agent had become an embarrassment to him and the public. This was a newfound wave of hypocrisy enshrouded in secrecy and deceit among the political figures in Lafourche Parish. The agent's dad was an elected official as well, compounding the complexity of my assignment.

On September 22, 1978, I set up surveillance on three subjects shooting ducks after hours, taking mottled ducks during closed season, taking over the limit of ducks, as well as wanton waste of migratory game birds. Official sunset on this date was 6:57 p.m. The last volley of shots from the individuals was 7:30 p.m. The reason for the late shooting law was to allow the ducks to roost without harassment.

As the three subjects exited the marsh, one was identified as the targeted agent. One subject had eight ducks, four over the limit. The over-limit subject stated that the agent, who was holding one duck, gave him some ducks. The lies and deception and their tangled web began to unravel as quickly as the words came out of their mouths. After writing citations to one subject, the suspended agent walked out of earshot with the other subject, whispering. This was an attempt to get their crooked story straight. The suspended agent came from the brief encounter to say the duck he was carrying belonged to the cited subject. The suspended agent desperately made an attempt to get that duck out of his hand, which was critical. Being an agent, he knew what it took to complete my case. The agent asked, "Did I f——up?" Then the agent changed his story stating the ducks were his. The agent stated I was being technical. I reminded the agent that he was sworn to uphold the law that he admitted to violating. The agent said he killed the teal duck he was holding in the last volley of shots at 7:30 p.m.

Later, I discovered through Major Boots that the suspended agent had hunted that morning as well—compounding his problem.

I was told not to sign my written investigation. This was a calculated move by the department to play their game. The department could satisfy their informant representative/congressman and, at the same time, satisfy the political connections of the agent. This statement also served as something of value over the agent's head to control him, if he came back to work.

Not to my surprise, nothing came out of the agent's complicity in the theft ring, nor were any charges filed in my duck investigation. This opened the door to his reemployment, which, in fact, did happen. The agent came back in full uniform and just gave me a sarcastic smile. The "I told you so" radiated from his body gestures. The same agent challenged me for the captain position and later resigned due to my promotion, never to return.

It was politics as usual in my job when, on December 14, 1983, at 1:40 p.m., I received a rare call from the Lafourche Parish sheriff (bomb victim). The sheriff was complaining about numerous problems. The one that concerned him the most was he was told by a wildlife violator that the agents gave instructions to the violator to bring the tickets to the sheriff to get fixed. The sheriff was screaming at me on the phone. There probably was an audience in the sheriff's office listening to him berate me. I told the sheriff that I would look into it. The sheriff gruffly said, "You don't have to look into it because it was you." I flat out called him a liar. There was no longer any reason for me to put up with his vulgar mouth. His mind was entrenched with the lie; therefore, I hung up on him while he continued to shout. That bold move made me feel good. The loudspeaker for his cronies to listen became silent, except for the dial tone. I calculated this move to embarrass the sheriff in front of his followers. I wanted to project an image that I would not take the harassment any longer. Christmas came in 1983, and I sang *Joy to the World*.

CHAPTER 9

Out with the Old, Back in with the Old

The Promise and the Lie

The old saying "Out with the old, in with the new" did not quite resonate with the shallow-minded voters in Louisiana. It was out with the old, back in with the old. The old governor, along with all his accomplices, were back in 1984. What a disappointment. How could I handle another four years of payback vengeance? All politicians bathed in their ignoble glory, unpredicted circumstances would alter the path of the future. I had to plot a strategy of survival, while still being effective as a wildlife supervisor/agent. My department smiled, and the colonel's statement "All dogs have their day" was about to come to fruition, so I thought. I often wondered what happened to the notarized affidavit I gave to the state police and attorney general's organized crime task force.

The Federal Bureau of Investigation's Introduction

The newspapers and media statewide were overflowing with news that the former governor, while a private attorney represented a subject arrested on a cocaine charge in Terrebonne Parish. While allegedly at least one other subject went to jail in the investigation, it was alleged that the district attorney of Terrebonne Parish dropped the cocaine charges against the former governor's client in exchange for an appointment to become secretary of Louisiana Department of Wildlife and Fisheries. The former governor said, "You can't do that because it is illegal." The former governor, to become governor elect, testified before the federal grand jury in New Orleans, Louisiana. The governor stated that Senator BB, in Terrebonne Parish, allegedly asked him to consider the district attorney for the secretary position. I have been sworn to testify in all sorts of actions during my career. The words "Please raise your right hand. Do you solemnly swear to tell the truth, the whole truth, and nothing but the truth, so help you God?" precedes every time one testifies. The truth can set you free as well as put you in jail.

On October 14, 1983, the district attorney of Terrebonne Parish was indicted by a federal grand jury in New Orleans Louisiana on four counts of perjury. One count allegedly surrounded the promising of the Louisiana Department of Wildlife and Fisheries secretary's position to the district attorney by the governor. Politics and public opinion can make or break you. There was an informed public of the inner workings of politics in Louisiana at its most grandiose moment. Lines were drawn and sides were taken. I was about to be thrown in the mix of wolves once again.

I never testified before the federal grand jury, but my impact, nonetheless, was an integral part of the indictment. My supervisor told me on January 4, 1984, that things were going to get really rough on me due to the indictment.

On January 24, 1984, I was informed by a representative of Louisiana Land Corporation that there was to be a meeting of LA Land, LA Terre Land Company, and Continental Land and Fur Company representatives along with the district attorney and my major. This meeting took place at 10:00 a.m. on January 25, 1984. The main topic of conversation was what to do with Roy Chauvin. My relationship with LA Land Corp and LA Terre Corp was excellent; therefore, I had a heads-up on the meeting.

On January 26, 1984, I was contacted by FBI agent J.D. He stated he needed to speak to me about threats made toward me at the meeting of January 25, 1984, with the district attorney and land representatives. Obviously, I had a friend at the meeting who took the threat seriously enough that he contacted the FBI. Thanks to my secret society of believers. Nothing of the nature of the threats was divulged to me by Agent Daigle other than they were serious. On January 27, 1984, my major confirmed he went to the meeting.

The Subpoena

On January 31, 1984, I met with FBI agent J.D., at his request, for two hours. During this meeting/investigation, he explored every credible threat made to me by the district attorney. All issues were covered: gill nets, shrimp, political, the district attorney's camp, etc. This was the first time I was informed I would be a witness in the perjury trial of the district attorney. It became quite evident that my 1982 affidavit was in the hands of the United States attorney and was used in the indictment of the district attorney.

The perjury trial of the district attorney began in February of 1984. On February 8, 1984, I was called by FBI agent F.C., who stated I was to come to New Orleans Federal District Courthouse right away to testify. "We want you to stay out of sight and wait in the United States attorney's office." I told FBI agent D.F. that I would not testify without a subpoena. I knew that I could not ignore the subpoena. It would force me to testify. I knew that the subpoena was a written document forever making me a witness against the district attorney and governor. The subpoena demanded my presence at 2 p.m. on February 8, 1984, in courtroom C-227 New Orleans, Louisiana, Federal District Court.

I hid out of sight, then at 6 p.m., assistant United States attorney, P.H., came into the office to talk to me. She stated, "All we want you to do is testify that the district attorney told you he would be secretary of the Louisiana Department of Wildlife and Fisheries." If the defense tries to go into other areas like the district attorney's camp, she said, "Dump on them, tell them everything, and don't stop." Harding said, "Don't tell anyone you are here and don't talk to anyone." It is my understanding that assistant United States attorney, P.H., drilled the district attorney on the stand asking if he made threats to me. Allegedly under oath, he said we were good friends. She questioned, "Did you threaten to fire him, transfer him, or change his status?"

On February 9, 1984, I went to court at 8:30 a.m. Assistant United States attorney, P.H., instructed me to go over my signed affidavit sworn to in 1982 concerning the district attorney. I was summoned to the courtroom but stopped outside by the assistant United States attorney and defense attorney, R.G. The assistant United States attorney stated defense counsel only wants to know if the district attorney told me after May 18, 1981, (heated meeting) that he would be secretary of Louisiana Department of Wildlife and Fisheries (LDWF). My answer was a truthful no. Under no circumstances did the defense attorney want me to testify before the jury. The defense knew that if I had the opportunity, I would blow his case wide open with my testimony. This indicated a fear of me.

Then the United States attorney, John Voltz, came into the courtroom. There were lots of arguing going on in court because the trial judge ruled my testimony inadmissible due to the time frame. I guess there is a statue of limitation on the truth when dealing with politics. On February 10, 1984, the district attorney, not to my surprise, was found not guilty. The outcome of the trial was insignificant to me because there was a clear message that even David could win against the Goliath. The district attorney's sails were tattered and torn. He never recovered to ride the political wave again. On February 27, 1984, the district attorney, in a newspaper article, revealed that he did not want to be secretary of the Louisiana Department of Wildlife and Fisheries. The question remains: Was that his decision, or the governor's? Shortly afterward, the district attorney decided not to run for reelection in 1985. Although he took several shots at the department, he was very, very careful not to aim at me personally.

On May 29, 1984, I had a meeting with LDWF heads to discuss my future. I told the department that I no longer feared any of their retaliation. At this meeting was Secretary Snake-Eyes, Colonel Ram, and Major Boots. They wanted to discuss my relationship with the indicted/acquitted district attorney. I was informed that there were rumors (lies) that the acquitted district attorney would be appointed deputy secretary of LDWF by the governor. They were pleading for my cooperation with the acquitted DA. This showed a sign of weakness on their part. Just as the warm sun shines on a cold snake, the warmer he gets the more likely he is to strike.

I reminded the attendees of the department how I was ostracized, a castaway, a leper lurking in the shadows. I also reminded them how they laughed at me when the acquitted district attorney in the front page of the Times-Picayune stated, "F——you and the horse you rode in on." I told the department staff that my horse and I survived that ordeal, and now the acquitted district attorney is standing next to his dead horse that wasn't going to be resurrected anytime soon. A very stressful chapter of my life had ended, but the best/worst was yet to come.

CHAPTER 10

New District Attorney Era

In Comes New District Attorney and Idealism

During the Advent of 1985 and the waning of 1984, many significant political events took place. The old governor was reelected and resurrected his corrupt agenda and cronies. In Terrebonne Parish, a new district attorney was elected. The election for district attorney took on a new characteristic in that I was courted for support due to my popularity with the statewide media. I was looked upon as an asset. I was very cautious meeting with two of the three candidates. They promised the moon and stars if elected—typical political rhetoric.

A young attorney with idealistic strategies won the election. He immediately brought me into his office stating that everything would change. He knew my philosophy, which he did not want to change at all. Instead, he wanted to build on that idealism. The new district attorney expected the law to be enforced as written. He did not want the confusion created by my department's interpretation of laws by invoking spirit of the law, which he felt led to favorable decisions only for a few. He vehemently stated anyone not enforcing the law will be charged with malfeasance.

The new district attorney asked me to prioritize significant problems. The two major issues were the enforcement of the inside-outside shrimp lines and the gill net issue. To inform the public of the changes, he set up commercial fishermen meetings at strategic locations. The district attorney said he wanted me to interpret the shrimp lines at the meetings. I told him the fishermen knew the lines on shrimping very well. The fishermen just won't stay outside due to the economic advantage of trawling in closed water. My department warned me that I did not work for the district attorney and I was to watch my mouth in dealing with the fishermen. The department, as well as elected officials, felt the district attorney could not carry through his promises. The politicians felt the public would eat the district attorney alive.

The first meeting took place in a local fishing community. Many of the fishermen were good, respectable people who wanted law enforcement. However, they felt it would never happen in Louisiana due to the political atmosphere. Approximately three hundred people attended the first meeting, which took place prior to the opening of the May shrimp season. There was a lot of hollering going on back and forth among the fishermen. The district attorney started the meeting by emphasizing his platform of fair and strict law enforcement. The district attorney stated he was there to answer questions so that there is no confusion if one is caught. The district attorney outlined the penalties for closed season shrimping. Agents can take your nets, shrimp, and even your boat, which all can be forfeited according to legislative actions that your senators and representatives approved. There were shouts of joy and as many boos coming from the rowdy audience. The district attorney stated he was turning the meeting over to me, and he suggested that fishermen should carefully listen because he would support my efforts 100 percent.

Also, I told the fishermen that they all knew who the problems were and where the problems existed. I told the fishermen that many of them call me to get help enforcing the shrimp line. I told them I could hear the frustration in their voices, but it was a new day, a good day, if things went as planned. The laws will be enforced fairly across the board. Don't call your politician if you are caught. That will only aggravate your situation. The audience of three hundred became quiet.

I told the crowd that I had explained to the district attorney not if someone crosses the line, but when someone crosses the line, he, the district attorney, would be tested. I told the crowd that the first case would be Caillou Boca, a notorious pass for close-season shrimping.

The crowd burst out in laughter shouting, "You're right, Chauvin, and what are you going to do?"

I told the crowd that "we would take the nets, shrimp, and a new twist, your boats."

The audience began shouting, "You can't do that!"

The district attorney stood up, saying, "Yes, he can, and he will follow the law."

I joked with the audience asking who was going to be first. After the meeting, some fishermen grumbled to me that they would not let me take their boats stating, "We will fight you."

Take or Don't Take the Boats

Meanwhile, my department stated that I was not to take orders from the district attorney. My orders were "Don't take the boats." I told Colonel Ram the district attorney will charge someone with malfeasance, and it was not going to be me. The politicians were on pins and needles, especially Representative BB who was now a Senator BB over my entire district. The colonel once again stated, "I am giving you a direct order not to take the boats." I requested the order in writing but never received the same. I told Colonel Ram I felt his order was illegal subjecting me to a criminal violation. "I will disobey a direct illegal order."

The district attorney heard of my current orders. He was furious. He wrote a blistering letter to Secretary Snake-Eyes informing the department of malfeasance in office charges as it pertained to enforcing the written law. The district attorney warned that agents were subject to sanctions of the law as well as those who give orders to violate the law. Threats continued from the department; however, they took on an apprehensive flare. Major Flip and Flop would blame the orders on Colonel Ram, who, in turn, blamed Secretary Snake-

Eyes, who deferred blame to the legal staff who invoked the spirit of the law in order to rationalize an illegal interpretation.

I attended meeting after meeting with the department, who felt intimidated by the district attorney, not really standing firm on their orders—in other words, cowards. I just sat watching them squirm like the nightcrawler worm ready to be eaten by a giant catfish. The whispered orders were "*Shh*, don't take the boats." In early May of 1985, I began to receive complaints about close-season shrimping at none other than Caillou Boca.

The Lady Shelley

On May 3, 1985, I was able to get the department floatplane to conduct a shrimp patrol. As we approached Caillou Boca, I could see a large number of boats pushing the line, but none were across. As we flew eastward, further inside the closed area, I observed a forty-five-foot-long vessel moving slowly along the north shore of the pass. The boat was clearly in closed waters and traveling further inside. I knew the boats pushing the line were watching as we circled. The vessel was named Lady Shelley. I could see the vessel was pulling two large trawls in closed season. I told the pilot to get down low so that I could instruct the captain to pick up his nets. The captain complied, but when he saw that the waters were too rough to land the plane, he, arrogantly, dropped his nets and continued to trawl further inside. I informed the agents in boats of our location while we circled Lady Shelley.

Old habits don't die. As I was circling the boat, I received a radio communication from Colonel Ram in Baton Rouge. The colonel asked if I was circling the Lady Shelley. I responded, "Yes." Colonel Ram asked what I was going to do. I told Colonel Ram I was going to follow the law. Colonel Ram stated he had a state representative from lower Lafourche Parish that wanted to talk to me before I did anything. Now, I was in an airplane, and this communication could be heard throughout the state. I informed Colonel Ram, by radio, that just as I don't work for the district attorney, nor do I work for the state representative. The colonel stated that the captain of the vessel had called the representative from the boat complaining that he could not make a living. Again, I was told, "Don't take the boat," by Colonel Ram.

The agents arrived as the vessel continued to shrimp. The agents boarded the vessel and stopped the captain. The pilot was able to land, and I boarded. At first, the captain complained that he did not know the location of the inside-outside shrimp line. I pointed to the thirty boats outside the line. The captain stated there were too many boats on the line. The captain stated he could not make any money competing with the thirty boats. The captain pointed to his catch saying he was catching ten times more shrimp than those fishing the line. The captain then asked if I had received a call from his representative. I did not answer. The captain stated, "I know he talked to you to leave me alone." I then informed the captain that we were taking his shrimp, nets, and his boat. The captain stated, "You can't do that. I'm going to have your job." I told the captain to "get in line if you wanted my job." The captain moaned and groaned as he tried to call the representative.

I got back into the plane when Colonel Ram called and asked about the case. I told the colonel that we seized the shrimp, nets, and the boat. Things went silent on the radio. The colonel asked about the boat and where I was going to bring it. I told him Cocodrie, Louisiana. The colonel dejectedly said, "Okay."

The district attorney called me asking what happened as he had received calls as well. I told the district attorney we seized the shrimp, nets, and boat. I told the district attorney the boat was approximately two miles inside the line with thirty boats on the line watching.

The district attorney said, "Okay. I can't believe he came inside."

I told the district attorney he did not know the fishermen as I did. I said, "We are going to fill up Cocodrie with boats."

He said, "Okay. Do it."

As a note, these vessels are equipped with sophisticated electronic equipment to determine the shrimp line. The shrimp line is described by law with both visual landmarks as well as coordinates. The equipment has a visual screen showing their exact location as it relates to the line. This equipment is so accurate, the fishermen can work within feet of the line.

The local media ran daily stories of our activities. One headline summed it up: Illegal Shrimping Risky in the Parish.

The department's retaliation was relentless. Meeting after meeting was called. I sat there saying nothing because I noted frustration on their part due to the lack of control of the district attorney. There were suggestions that I toned down the district attorney's aggressive tactics. The department stated he could not do it without me. I reminded the department about their wishy-washy stance promulgated by whoever was in office. It was obvious that the department was intimidated by the district attorney, but they did not have any power to control him.

CHAPTER 11

Grand Isle, Louisiana

Grand Isle Debacle

The department was at wit's end on how to deal with me. Their new plan was to strip me of my authority over the agents, having the agents answer directly to Colonel Ram and Secretary Snake-Eyes. Everyone was taping conversations. Only three agents remained loyal to me. The plane was taken from me, my checks were lost in the mail, and my step increases were held up.

As a result of the strict enforcement of the shrimp line in Terrebonne, the good residents of Lafourche Parish wanted the same. The fishermen wanted strict enforcement at Caminada and Barataria Pass in Grand Isle, Louisiana, which was in Jefferson Parish. At Caminada Pass, politicians wanted enforcement to allow the fishermen to close-season shrimp to a set of power lines well within the closed area and legal line. Since the area had little or no enforcement before I became in charge, I decided to set up meetings with the fishermen. Accompanying me also was the media attached to my hip for protection.

Grand Isle is a small remote island, one way in and one way out, bordered by the Gulf of Mexico. It was a haven for criminals dating back to pirate Jean Lafitte. The seclusion empowered the residents to feel like they had their own country with its own set of rules. It is my understanding that Whitney Bulgar, of the FBI's most wanted list, hid there for ten years.

My first meeting was held in Galliano, Louisiana. Caminada Pass was the key issue. The fishermen asked about the shrimp line at Caminada Pass. I quoted the law using coordinates and land points. The fishermen asked why they were allowed to fish to the power lines and beyond. I told the fishermen that I had been given orders to lie to the fishermen about the line and give to the power lines. The fishermen asked who gave these orders. I responded by saying Colonel Ram and Major Flip and Flop. The fishermen were infuriated. The Daily Comet newspaper in Lafourche Parish had headquarters in Baton Rouge running for cover as the reporter sought comments. Major Flip and Flop, confused, told the truth stating, "We told Chauvin to give to the power lines."

On July 31, 1985, a meeting was held on Grand Isle. Heated discussion came as a result of the meeting as well as threats to run me out of Grand Isle. I told the fishermen that we would enforce the law as written as I handed out maps of the line. I reminded the fishermen of the May 7, 1984, meeting on Grand Isle, citing the raid that followed the meeting, resulting in twenty-one boats being seized on May 15, 1984.

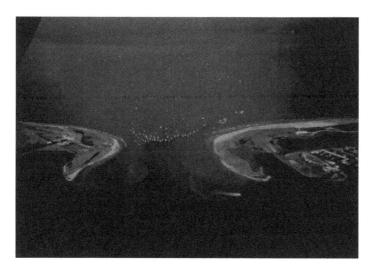

The Judges

On October 4, 1984, the twenty-one closed-season shrimp cases following the May 7, 1984, meeting in Grand Isle went to trial in Jefferson Parish. Two judges were handling the cases. Prior to the trial, the judges called me, the defense attorney, and the two prosecutors into chambers. Judge Powerline stated, "I will not find anyone guilty for fishing to the power lines." This judge stated that there was an agreement with the governor and Secretary Snake-Eyes to allow fishermen to fish to the power lines during closed season. I explained to the judge that neither he nor I have the authority to give to the power lines in violation of the law.

The defense attorneys stated that their clients would plead guilty upon condition that legislation would be introduced in the next session to place the line at the power lines. Not to my surprise, no legislation was introduced. As the defendants began their guilty pleas, the judge went ballistic and shouted, "I am dismissing all charges!"

The department's solution to the problem came on August 7, 1985, when I was relieved of my duties in Grand Isle. One of my disloyal subordinates was placed in charge. I did not fight the decision, which proved to be a good one.

As a result of my departure, the disloyal agents became pawns in the political game in Grand Isle and asked for my help. On February 6, 1986, the two agents were subpoenaed by Judge I'm Sorry on a rule to show cause on why he should not hold them in contempt. I went to court with the agents. We met in the judge's chambers. The judge seemed very stressed out, saying he would like to ask the agent a few questions under oath. I explained to the judge, in the absence of an attorney, the agents would invoke the Fifth Amendment against self-incrimination. The judge needed answers, so he just asked questions in chambers. Judge I'm Sorry asked if he had a problem with the agents and the LDWF. He heard the agents were upset with his court, and he could not take the criticism resulting in contempt charges. The judge stated that he did not agree with the shrimp line at Grand Isle, but he did not have the authority to change the line. The judge said it was a definite violation to fish to the power lines.

He promised total cooperation in the future but could not speak for Judge Powerline. It was my understanding that this judge was allegedly under federal investigation for improprieties while performing his duties. It is my understanding that this judge later resigned.

Certain things never stay behind closed doors. My guardian angel was there once again.

Judge Powerline remained obstinate and defiant. He got what he wanted when I was pulled out of Grand Isle. My stand created the proposal of House Bill 1676 of the 1986 legislature addressing the shrimp lines at Cominada Pass and Barataria Pass in Grand Isle, Louisiana. It was now legal to fish to the power lines. A decision, which later, the fishermen on Grand Isle would regret.

On September 9, 1985, I was called to a meeting, which centered around my disobeying orders to give to the power lines in Grand Isle. Colonel Ram stated, "There are some things you cannot put in writing. You know what we want." I was once again ordered to meet with Senator BB to discuss the situation. On September 24, 1985, I asked for a meeting with unhappy Senator BB. He declined but chose to chastise me over the phone—déjà vu. He brought up all sorts of trivial grievances, but in a submissive, defeated tone, he stated that he would sponsor a bill in the next legislative session to change the shrimp line to the power lines (House Bill 1676). This conversation was about as productive as a gnat eying an elephant for a takedown meal.

The September 9 meeting was followed by a registered letter stating that the meeting was an official verbal reprimand. This was typical of Colonel Ram's cowardly acts to send the letter after the meeting. In return, on September 14, 1985, I sent a registered letter to Colonel Ram. The letter recanted the problems in Grand Isle and the politics in general as it pertained to my job. If a verbal reprimand, I requested a hearing to produce witnesses and documents to serve as my defense. Two days later, I received a letter from Colonel Ram saying that the meeting was not an official verbal reprimand, rather, it was a discussion of my performance. "This will not be placed in your file."

On February 28, 1985, the governor and five associates were indicted by a federal grand jury in New Orleans. The indictments were over state certificates on proposed hospital construction. All were charged with violating the Racketeer Influenced and Corrupt Organization Act (RICO). The governor was never convicted, but he realized his vulnerability.

EXHIBIT 16

State of Louisiana

DEPARTMENT OF WILDLIFE AND FISHERIES
POST OFFICE BOX 15570
BATON ROUGE, LA 70895

504-925-3617

CERTIFIED MAIL
RETURN RECEIPT REQUESTED

September 6, 1985

Captain Roy Chauvin
Route 1, Box 5041
Gibson, LA   70356

Dear Captain Chauvin:

This is to confirm my orders conveyed to you by Major ████████ to report
to my office on Monday, September 9, 1985, at 10:30 A.M.

You are to report to the 3rd Floor of the Tres' Bien Building in the
Bon Marche Mall in Baton Rouge.

Sincerely,

Colonel ████████
Chief-Enforcement Division

RAM:src

cc: Major ████████
cc: ████████

September 14, 1985

To: Colonel ████████

From: Captain Ray Chauvin

Subject: Response as requested pursuant to the meeting of September 9, 1985 in Baton Rouge

Dear ████████,

    I am writing this statement in response to our meeting of September 9, 1985 at your office in Baton Rouge. In addition to yourself, Major ████████ (my immediate supervisor) and I attended the meeting. At first, I thought that this meeting would be general in nature, but upon returning home from the meeting I received a certified letter concerning the meeting. Also on September 10, 1985 I met with Major ████████ and asked him the specific nature of the meeting. Major ████████ informed me that the meeting was an "OFFICIAL VERBAL REPRIMAND". I am not sure at this point whether or not the meeting was an official reprimand. Therefore I feel that I should address subjects discussed at the meeting.

    First of all, I would like to apologize to all those whom I am supposed to have offended. My actions, my intentions, and my desires have always centered around doing the best job I could do so that my Department would be proud of me. I would never purposely undermine the sincere efforts of my Department as it relates to the public and wildlife. Furthermore, I will do everything within my power to respect the wishes of this Department as it relates to my duties as Captain of District 8B. Personally, I have a great deal of pride in dealing with my profession and have always thrived on doing a better job year after year. I am not trying to be Number 1...just better. The 100% effort that I always give an assignment is often misinterpreted as being arrogant and superior. For this misconception I am sorry, but I cannot seem to be able to change people's minds.

68

The meeting of September 9, 1985 was riddled with misunderstandings, suppositions and inuendoes. Hopefully, I will be able to shed some light on our dilema. First of all you said that I was trying to separate District 8B from the rest of the State. I feel that this is untrue. Region 8 (of which you were Captain) has always been separated, not by choice, from the rest of the State. We always have more going on and we are always expected to do more. Then, the more we do, the more attention we attract. With recognition in hand, resentment follows. District 8B is a prototype of Region 8. We lead all districts in the State every year in one important statistic...work and the high quality of work...as each monthly computer print-out shows. To achieve this success takes team work from all of the agents. True, some are not always happy, but they still have to work. All I ask is that they give the State an hour's work for an hour's pay. I have never threatened any agents. I have never been unavailable to agents. I have never let others do my work and furthermore, I have never treated one differently from the other. I feel as though I have to be strict in order to avoid the illegal and corrupt practices which cost four agents their jobs two years ago. This (fact) did irreparable damage to our public image, which will take years to improve.

This brings us to our next topic of discussion, which was my relationship with the news media. Personally, I feel that the media is an effective tool, which if used properly, not selfishly for one's own ego, can educate the public to make our job easier. I am told that I am not "gagged", but my views have to reflect that of the Department. The particular article cited was the one in the Daily Comet on July 31, 1985 concerning "shrimp enforcement" in Caminada Pass of Jefferson Parish. In order to clarify this problem I will have to give a brief synopsis of the events which led up to the article.

Approximately a year and a half ago I was ordered to court along with several other agents to testify against twenty-one (21) defendants, who were caught butterflying during closed season at Caminada Pass. Before the trial Lieutenant ████████████, Lieutenant ███████ and I were brought into the chambers of Judge ███████ and Judge ███████. Also present were two prosecutors and two defense attorneys. Judge ███████ said that we could not clearly define the line and told me that he would not find anyone guilty from the powerlines to the gulf. I told the judges that I did not have the authority to change the line and that he (Judge ███████) would have to speak to Mr. ███████. Well, just prior to the 1985 Fall shrimp season problems began to develop in the Caminada Pass area. At first it was suggested that I give the fishermen fishing rights to the powerlines, a boundary which is approximately one-half mile inside the "inside-outside" line as described in 56:495. Agents always use discretion, though not politically motivated, in order to make a good case. I never ordered my agents to "give to the powerlines", but I did tell them the powerlines was what the Department wanted. On July 29, 30, and 31, 1985, I was ordered to give to the powerlines by Major ███████, who said the

orders came from you, Colonel ████████ I asked and am still asking
for those orders in writing. I was refused the orders in writing
on July 31, 1985 by Major ███████████. Later that night I attended
a commercial fishermen's meeting in Galliano, Louisiana. I tried
to avoid the Caminada Pass issue, but I was asked "why was Caminada
Pass the only place that somebody can shrimp in closed season". I
responded as Major ███████████ instructed me to do...Quote: I HAVE
BEEN INSTRUCTED BY MY SUPERIORS TO LET THEM FISH TO THE POWERLINE...
Unquote. Major ███████████ did remind you at the meeting of September 9,
1985 that he had instructed me to answer the way I did to the fishermen.

This was the first time in my career that I was given a direct
"illegal" order. I feel that all discretion was stripped from the
agents and that the potential for violence was inevitable. All of
the agents felt that someone would get hurt at Caminda Pass if the
inconsistent enforcement continued. I am not sure why you took the
stand you did at Caminada, but I feel that the pressure of Judge ████████
was felt by all. I hope that his type of situation never develops
again because I do not feel that I can morally or legally do what was
expected of me. I am asking you not to place me in that situation again.

The final phase of our meeting was the most discouraging of all.
The topic of conversation was my relationship with District Attorney
███████████ and Houma City Court Judge ███████████. I really don't
know what to think about this problem. I am being portrayed as a
"vindictive-egotistical" agent who is lashing out at the Department with
my every action.

On or about April 22, 1985 I received a phone call from Lt. Col.
████████ concerning the D.A.'s request on seizing shrimp boats.
All Lt. ███████████ told me was ... Quote: "GO BY THE LAW...BURT
WANTS YOU TO GO BY THE LAW". Well I figured that the problem was
solved. It was the D.A.'s request that we seize boats. On May 2,1985
I was ordered by Maj. ███████████ NOT to seize boats. Major ████████
said that you, Colonel ████████ did not want me to seize any boats. On
May 3, 1985, I caught the boat "LADY SHELLEY" trawling and double
rigging in inside waters during CLOSED SEASON. As so ordered, I did
not seize the boat. However, later that afternoon I was asked by
the D.A. why we did not seize the boat. I informed him that I was
obeying orders from the Department. On the afternoon of May 3, 1985
Major ███████████ informed me that he had received orders from you, Col.
Montet, to seize the boat and that was after the D.A. had spoken to
you directly. Therefore, it was you who gave the final order to seize
the boats. I seized the boat "LADY SHELLEY" on May 4, 1985 at 9:00 A.M.
I was following the chain of command and was doing what I was ordered
to do by my Department.

I regret that you feel that I have influenced the D.A. and City Judge against our Department. I am being blamed for circumstances and actions of people over which I have no control. You told me that the entire legislative delegation is upset with District Attorney ████████ and that I should have a meeting with Senator ████████ I think that this set of circumstances is very unfortunate because I am only trying to cooperate with the District Attorney and the City Judge in upholding the law. I absolutely do not want another ████████ type of cooperation between me and the Department. I feel like I am caught in the middle. I do not feel that it is fair and just to condemn me for doing a good job for the Department. In order to put an end to RUMORS, such as my controlling the District Attorney and the City Judge I am requesting a meeting with the entire Legislative Delegation of Terrebonne and Lafourche Parishes, District Attorney ████████, City Judge ████████, Secretary ████████ ████████e, Colonel ████████t, Lt. Col. ████████, Maj. ████████ and I, Captain Roy Chauvin. I contend that I am not "the problem" but the victim of the problem. I am willing to do whatever the Department wants in order to best serve the public and wildlife. My only regret is that I was hoping that my Department, to who I am loyal, would share with me in the cooperative atmosphere which surrounds a working system in District 8B. Without this cooperation and understanding we all stand to lose. None of us has problems that cannot be solved with the right kind of cooperation and understanding.

If this is an official verbal reprimand, I object that I was not timely notified nor notified of the official nature of the meeting. If this meeting was official in nature, I respectfully request an opportunity to fully answer the charges that were to be the subject of the meeting including a fair opportunity to produce witnesses to explain the situations at issue. Further, I desire that I be fully informed of all complaints in order that the appropriate matters be addressed. If this was an official verbal reprimand I would like a copy of all tapes, letters, notes, statements and any other materials upon which you based your reprimand. This will also help guide me to avoid problems in the future.

Finally, after due consideration of this response, please advise me in writing as to the status of this matter and how it will affect my civil service record. In particular, if this is to adversely affect my record, I desire to be so notified in order that I may take the appropriate steps to appeal and/or respond to the complaints at issue and action taken by this Department.

I personally feel that the matters which have been discussed with me and of which you complain are not the proper subject of any sort of disciplinary action or other action which ████ affect my status under the civil service laws of this State. These matters appear to be arising as a result of "politics" in the Department and outside

the Department. In order to avoid any further confusion on the policies
and positions of this Department, I would appreciate the manner in
which I am to handle my job, be put in writing. I am sorry to make
this request but due to confusion on these matters from the past, I
feel that these matters must now be put in writing in order to avoid
problems and discrepancies.

   As I have said earlier, it is my only desire to do my job and
enforce the laws of this State. I want to do my job in a professional
manner and to be an asset to this Department. It is my hope that
all concerned can resolve the issues at hand so that this Department
and the people of this State can be better served and the image
of our Department improved.

                                        Sincerely,

                                        Capt. Roy Chauvin

                                        Captain Roy Chauvin

cc: Burton Angelle
       Major

State of Louisiana

DEPARTMENT OF WILDLIFE AND FISHERIES
ENFORCEMENT DIVISION
P O BOX 15570
BATON ROUGE, LOUISIANA 70895
504/925-4912

October 25, 1985

M E M O R A N D U M

TO: CAPTAIN ROY CHAUVIN

FROM: COLONEL ████████

SUBJECT: CORRESPONDENCE

Please refer to your correspondence to me dated September 14, 1985, relative to "RESPONSE AS REQUESTED PURSUANT TO THE MEETING OF SEPTEMBER 9, 1985 IN BATON ROUGE".

The meeting on September 9, 1985 in Baton Rouge attended by you, Major ████████ and me was not an "official verbal reprimand". I requested that you and Major ████ meet with me to discuss your performance as Captain of District 8-C. Furthermore, I do not have the authority to issue official reprimands. That authority is limited to the Secretary of the Department of Wildlife and Fisheries.

Your correspondence dated September 14, 1985 will be considered a confirmation of our meeting. It, along with this response, will be filed in your Enforcement Division Personnel files. If will not be filed in the Personnel Office files and does not affect your Civil Service status.

Should you need any additional clairification regarding this matter, please advise.

Ram/crl

Sept. 29, 1985

To: Colonel ███████████
From: Captain Roy Chauvin ████
Subject: Meeting with Senator ████

Dear ████████████

As per your request of September 9, 1985 to have a
meeting with Senator ██████, I have complied.
Senator ██████ and I spoke briefly on Sept. 24, 1985.
In the future I would ask that you, Col. ██████
shield me and my men from such abusive, non-productive
and intimidating circumstances. I feel that these
meetings interfere with my duties as the same relate
to enforcement of the Laws of the State of Louisiana.
Furthermore, I feel that any change in the Civil
Service status of me or any of my men will be a direct
result of the political confusion.

Sincerely,

Capt Roy Chauvin

Captain Roy Chauvin

cc: Major ████████████
Secretary ████████████

CHAPTER 12

Gill Nets

Right to Fish

As we turned the corner in 1985 and began a new year, one controversy reared its ugly head that divided the state like no other issue. The problem was a user group dilemma that pitted commercial fishermen, historically taken care of by Governor Rico and his administration against sportsmen, who, in the past, lacked direction and perseverance. Commercial fishermen always had the advantage in that they claimed fishing was a way of life all the way back to Jesus's time. The fishermen also claimed it was a right rather than a privilege to fish. The sportsman, on the other hand, said fishing was a privilege rather than a right. Commercial fishermen follow the old rule: Call the politician to get enforcement off their backs. However, things were changing. The lenient and vague laws passed in the legislature to protect the resources were no longer acceptable. The biologists, who made recommendations, often compromised their findings in favor of inept legislation, not wanting to upset the hand that fed them. The gill net issue became an uncompromising user group battle—you or me. The commercial fishermen wanted it all. The Gulf Coast Conservation Association said, "Okay, if that is the game you want to play, then let's go for it."

My area, as usual, was one of the most prolific areas of resource; therefore, there were more confrontations between commercial fishermen and sportsmen. The center of controversy was the use of gill nets, which was a traditional method to take fish. A gill net is like a fence, some 1,200 feet or longer, into which fish were herded and caught by the gills. Thousands of pounds of fish could be caught in a single set. Our laws were so lax, and the resource so vast that out-of-state netters came to reap the benefits arising from poor management.

Right off the bat, the sportsmen targeted monofilament gill nets, which were an easy, light, effective tool for the fishermen. There was no compromise on who would win. The GCCA had massive numbers, most of which were voters, thus, causing the raised eyebrows of many politicians seeking election and reelection. How were the politicians going to dance around this issue? Commercial fishermen stuck to their old guns and ways, which was soon to become a dinosaur. A bill was introduced in the legislature to do away with monofilament gill nets. It passed—strike one for the commercial fishermen. The GCCA compromised by imposing a limit on recreational fishermen of fifty fish. There was no recreational limit on fish prior to this legislation.

Then the issue came up on unattended gill nets. The GCCA targeted these nets because, at any given time, hundreds of the nets were placed on points of land and indiscriminately caught fish by the thousands. Often, these nets were left out too long, and the fish would die, floating, sending a stench across Sportsman's Paradise (the motto on Louisiana's license plates). Legislation passed stating that unattended gill nets were illegal—strike two for the uncompromising fishermen.

The Petition

The issue became the definition of unattended. In all their wisdom, the Department of Wildlife and Fisheries and the politicians said leave the fishermen alone. Don't enforce the law. Those comments forced the GCCA's hand. The first week the law went into effect, we picked up thirty-four unattended gill nets in one day. I was criticized by my department and politicians. The GCCA got wind of the criticism and took action. The statewide president of the GCCA, C.A., and the Terrebonne Parish chapter president, J.W., drew up a petition on February 14, 1985. To summarize the petition, it stated, "We the undersigned, concerned citizens, are supporters of enforcement of the law…in District 8 B… We are deeply troubled by the political interference of these processes… It is not proper for politicians to interfere with those positions, and persons in those positions… Therefore, we demand that the political pressure be directed toward the enforcement agents of District 8-B…and the District Attorney's of Terrebonne and Lafourche parishes, in an attempt to prevent them from doing their jobs… Be stopped immediately and permanently. Certified names with addresses."

On March 24, 1986, I was called to a meeting at Baton Rouge headquarters. Those attending the meeting were Secretary Snake-Eyes, Colonel RAM, and Major Flip and Flop. Secretary Snake-Eyes opened the meeting by demanding that I write a letter to the GCCA president, C.A., stating that no political pressure was being placed on me by the LDWF, the administration, and politicians. "If you refuse, I am going to replace you." Then Secretary Snake-Eyes made a cold, chilling threat that had future implications. "Are you willing to lose everything you have for what you believe in?" I told him not to test me or he would lose. He stated, "You are always talking about the corrupt politics in Baton Rouge. Well, put up, or shut up." I was sick and tired of their threats. As a result of Secretary Snake-Eyes's statement to put up or shut up, I began an investigation on specific acts of corruption by politicians and the department. This document with irrefutable evidence would serve as my answer to the GCCA petition.

Soon afterward, we made hundreds of cases of unattended gill nets. The department's interpretation of the law was to leave fishermen alone if they were in the vicinity of the nets. The vicinity could mean the fishermen were at home drinking coffee. The department's attorney said we are going by the spirit of the law. I told the attorney that I could read the definition of unattended, but I can't see the spirit. I told the department that interpretation would lead to selective enforcement and grounds for a civil rights violation.

On January 17, 1986, District Attorney of Terrebonne Parish wrote to Secretary Snake-Eyes a scathing nine-page letter outlining what he expected from law enforcement. One section of the letter dealt with enforcement of unattended and untagged gill nets.

"If an authorized fisherman or the owner of the net is not physically present, the net should be considered unattended.

"All untagged nets should be picked up.

"An application for a gill net license will not be accepted."

Agents loyal to the department followed one set of orders, while the agents loyal to me followed the law.

On May 1, 1986, District Attorney had had enough selective enforcement. In open court, he instructed Assistant District Attorney John Walker to cite the cases of selective enforcement.

CHAPTER 13

The Epistle

It was obvious that the department and politicians were not going to stop their relentless and unfounded attacks. My new strategy of putting things in writing irritated the department. If the meetings were serious enough, I would send letters via certified mail with a return receipt. I was ordered to stop putting things in writing due to the fact that the contents fell into the hands of the public and the feared media.

In my official civil service rating of 1985 and 1986, the department alleged that I was being influenced by outside parties—District Attorney. As a result, I was undermining the efforts of the department in order to create my own domain.

To counter the rating, I filed an official grievance against the department employing Louisiana civil service regulations. There were specific rules and timelines, which the department had to adhere to. It was similar to a legal proceeding with witnesses, affidavits, and I was even entitled to have an attorney present at all steps. I chose never to have an attorney.

In the first step of the grievance, I was told by Major Flip and Flop to proceed to the second step.

In the second step, the colonel would investigate and place in writing his results. In my certified letter to Colonel Ram, on July 24, 1986, I asked that the colonel recuse, or remove himself from this step due to his biased actions.

Corruption Brought to the Forefront

I asked to go to the third step of grievance procedures in which the secretary would chair the grievance hearing. Then on October 9, 1986, outside the parameters of the grievance procedures policy, the secretary set up a hearing. In attendance was Secretary Snake-Eyes; human resources head, and staff attorneys, Attorney Spirit of the Law and Attorney Go Along.

Secretary Snake-Eyes was very upset at the meeting. In my answer to the GCCA petition, I compiled a 270-page document with fifty-one exhibits of corruption enhanced by irrefutable evidence. I sent this document via Federal Express through an attorney friend (GCCA) to Secretary Snake-Eyes. Secretary Snake-Eyes began the meeting by shouting. I told Secretary Snake-Eyes that, in lieu of an attorney, I would be taping the proceedings, placing my recorder on the desk. Secretary Snake-Eyes asked Attorney Spirit of the Law if that was legal. Spirit of the Law stated it was legal for me to tape the proceedings.

Then Secretary Snake-Eyes started the hearing/meeting by throwing my 270-page document on the table stating, "What is this? The epistle according to Roy Chauvin?" I explained to Secretary

Snake-Eyes that on March 24, 1986, he ordered me to put up, or shut up.

"This document was my answer to your order to write GCCA president, Cornell Arceneaux, on the politics in my job."

Secretary Snake-Eyes stated, "What do you want me to do with it?"

I replied, "I don't care."

Then Secretary Snake-Eyes stated, "I am a politician, who makes political decisions. Do you think there is no pressure on me to make favorable decisions? Why don't you take my job?"

I responded by saying, "Obviously there was politics." But it was his job to shield me from the politics rather than participate. I stated it was okay for the administration to be political. I don't want to be a politician. "I will fight you every step of the way to be fair and honest."

Secretary Snake-Eyes replied, "Are you saying I am dishonest?"

I said, "I did not say that, but your political decisions are dishonest, and they serve only a few. That is not fair."

Media Blitz

The meeting/hearing ended. I told Secretary Snake-Eyes that he violated civil service rules as they pertain to my grievance. I would follow up this hearing in writing, and I intended to appeal his lack of a decision. "Civil service will be informed that you chose to ridicule me over the 270-page document." It is my understanding that two days later, Secretary Snake-Eyes suffered a heart attack.

On December 1, 1986, I answered Secretary Snake-Eyes's hearing letter of October 30, 1986. My eleven-page letter outlined my concerns.

The 270-page document wound up in the hands of the media. Those taking the lead were Mike Cook, Baton Rouge Advocate, and Bob Marshall, New Orleans Times-Picayune, as well as many other media outlets. The document was sent to the United States attorney's offices in Baton Rouge and New Orleans. The document was also sent to GCCA president, C.A.

As a result of the document, I was called to the US attorney's office in Baton Rouge. US Attorney R.L. had been conducting an investigation, which resulted in twelve criminal counts against Major Gopher in Baton Rouge headquarters.

G.C.C.A. OF HOUMA-TERREBONNE

February 25, 1986

Dear Fellow GCCA Member:

It has been brought to my attention and to the attention of several other concerned citizens of Terrebonne and Lafourche Parishes that there exists ever increasing political pressure on the Wildlife and Fisheries Enforcement Agents assigned to Terrebonne and Lafouche Parishes which is hampering their effectiveness and ability to enforce the laws in existence to preserve and protect our wildlife and fisheries. One area of particular interest to us as recreational fisherman is the interference with the agents in the enforcement of the unattended net law. This interference is coming from positions of authority within the Department of Wildlife and Fisheries who are receiving political pressure to interfere with the enforcement efforts of the agents.

As you are I am sure aware, we have one of the most effective enforcement districts in the state and the future of our preservation efforts of wildlife and fisheries is to have an effective enforcement agency to enforce the laws. There are certain special interest groups and politicians who are trying to undermine the effectiveness of the agents in our district and it is up to us as concerned citizens first and recreational fishermen second to lend and show our support for honest and objective enforcement of the law.

One of the methods we are attempting to use to show support of the citizens of Terrebonne and Lafourche Parishes for honest and objective enforcement of the law by the enforcement agents of Terrebonne and Lafourche Parishes is a petition, a copy of which is enclosed. It is requested that you sign this petition and obtain as many signatures as you can from people who share your concerns on this subject. When you have gotten as many signatures as possible, please return the petition to me at P. O. Box 5095, Houma, Louisiana 70361 or the state office in Baton Rouge.

I also urge you to voice your opinion and concern to our elected officials as soon as possible and urge anyone else you can persuade to do the same.

If we do not show support for the efforts of the enforcement agents of our parishes and the District Attorneys of our parishes, matters are just going to get worse. Now is the time to act.

P.O. BOX 5095 • HOUMA, LOUISIANA 70361 • TELEPHONE: (504) 868-2333

P E T I T I O N

We, the undersigned, concerned citizens of Terrebonne and Lafourche Parishes are supporters of the enforcement of the law by the Enforcement Agents of District 8B of Region 8 of the Louisiana Department of Wildlife and Fisheries and the prosecution of violations by the office of District Attorney in both parishes.

We are deeply troubled by the political interference of these processes that has been taking place.

The proper forum for addressing alleged or feared inequities of the law, whether it be concerning wildlife and fisheries or not, is in the Legislature which enacts the law, and the courts which interpret and apply the sanctions of the law. It is not proper for politicians to interfere with those positions, and persons in those positions, charged with the enforcement of the law.

Therefore, we demand that the political pressure being directed toward the Enforcement Agents of District 8B of Region 8 of the Louisiana Department of Wildlife and Fisheries and the District Attorneys of Terrebonne and Lafourche Parishes in an attempt to prevent them from doing their jobs to the best of their ability, be stopped immediately and permanently.

NAME: ADDRESS:

_____   _____

_____   _____

_____   _____

_____   _____

_____   _____

_____   _____

_____   _____

placed on unsupervised probation for one year, during which time period he cannot hunt alligators. (Exhibits 49, 50, 51)

Mr. ███████, the list goes on and on....Joey ██████, Dale ██████, Ronald ██████████), Chris ███████████, and Gervais ██████....just to mention a few. It is documented that I attended a meeting on March 24, 1986 in which Major ████████, Col. ████████ and yourself were present. I stated that a great deal of the problem was Col. ████████. Also at this meeting I requested that you shield me from the politics and the detrimental effects of the same as previously cited. Mr. ████████, at this meeting you requested that I write a letter to Cornell Arceneaux, State President of the Gulf Coast Conservation Association, stating that I have never received any political pressure from anyone inside or outside of the Department of Wildlife and Fisheries to offset the GCCA petition. Mr. ████████, I would like for this statement to serve as proof that various degrees of political pressure and influence does exist within the Department of Wildlife and Fisheries. Mr. ████████, you stated that if I did not write the letter to Cornell Arceneaux to offset the GCCA petition that you would, personally, remove the problem in Terrebonne and Lafourche Parishes. Mr. ████████, in light of the above statement I do not think that this is fair, because my only goal is to find JUSTICE.

Please be advised that in my statement it is quite possible that State and Federal violations of the law have been committed and I intend to g ive any and all information to the proper authorities for possible legal action.

Also, please be advised I feel that my Civil Rights as a citizen of the United States of America and the civil rights of some of my agents have been violated. Therefore, I am currently seeking the advice of numerous attorneys in order that I may file appropriate civil action with respect to my claim.

Captain Roy Chauvin, Jr.
Supervisor of Terrebonne and Lafourche Parishes
Enforcement Division Louisiana Department of Wildlife and Fisheries

Capt. Roy J. Chauvin Jr. 2758
July 24, 1986

85

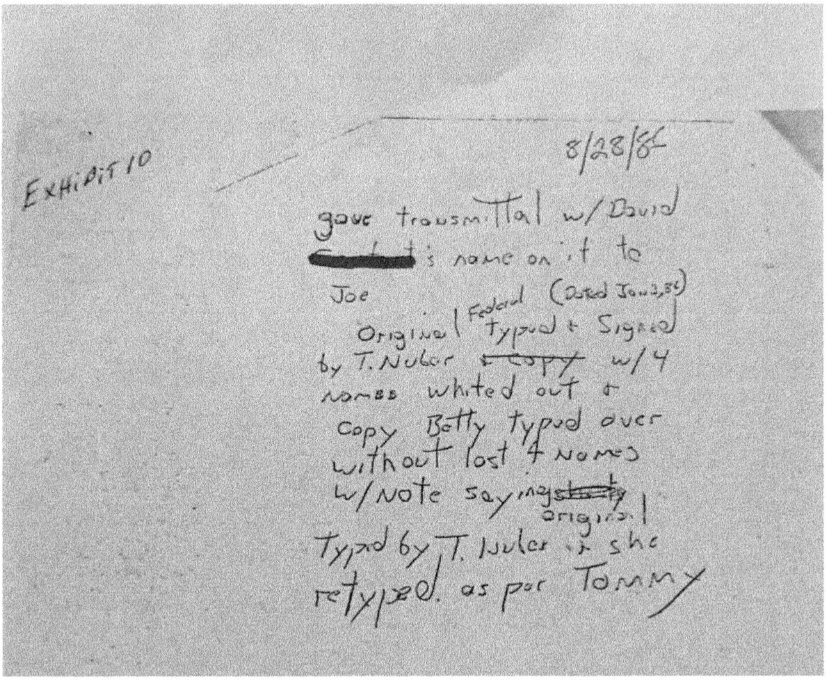

EXHIBIT 10

8/28/8-

gave transmittal w/ David
████'s name on it to
Joe
Original Federal (dated Jan 2,86)
Typed + Signed
by T. Nuber Copy w/ 4
names whited out +
copy Betty typed over
without last 4 names
w/ Note saying original
Typed by T. Nuber + she
retyped. as per Tommy

86

LOUISIANA
DEPARTMENT OF WILDLIFE AND FISHERIES
ENFORCEMENT DIVISION

Region No. 8B Parish Code No. 29 Employee No. 4175 Code No. 471

State of Louisiana _Sta. & Ins._ Judicial 17th Court District
Parish of

SUMMONS

The undersigned, being duly sworn upon his oath deposes and says,
on the 19 day of March 19 83 at 10:30 P M.

Name MincK T. Percle

Address RT 3 Box 622E

City Thibodaux State La. 70301

Date of Birth 01-0163 Occupation Carpenter

Race W Sex M Height 5'11" Weight 135 Hair Br Eyes Brn

Dr. Lic. No. 602631624 did unlawfully No
Boat Numbers

Namely at (location) Grand Bayou
Parish of violation Lafourche

and did then and there commit the following offense. RS 31:313

License No.
Fishing _____ Hunting _____ Seized Game _____

Tag No. _____ Equipment _____
Boat Reg. LA-6130-NT Exp. Date 22-25-85

Veh. Lic. No. _____ State and Year _____
The undersigned further states that he has just and reasonable grounds
to believe, and does believe, that the person named above committed the
offense herein set forth, contrary to law of the State of Louisiana in such
case made and provided and against the peace and dignity of the same.
C. Cook 4175
Signature and Employee No.

Sworn to before me this _____ day of _____ 19 ___

_____
Notary or Ex Officio Notary

COURT APPEARANCE:

Date 10 days Time _____ AM PM Ph. _____

at Pay fine Lafourche Sheriff Off
I understand the terms and conditions of this citation and promise to
appear at the time and place shown above. Failure to appear will be cause
for a warrant issued for my arrest.

Signed By Pat Percle
THIS SIGNATURE IS NOT AN ADMISSION OF GUILT

C02499

LEON L. BORNE, JR.
State Representative
District 55
P.O. Drawer 1500
Thibodaux, LA 70302

Captain Ray Chauvin
Rt. 1 Box 5041
Cut Off, LA
70356

87

Leon L. Borne, Jr.
State Representative

Captain Chauvin —

This man received these numbers the night before your agent saw fit to issue this citation. I believe that discretion would have deemed it inadviseable to issue anything but a warning. Please have these charges dropped —

FEDERAL

CITATION NUMBER	DEFENDANT'S NAME	OFFENSE	ARRESTING AGENT
C-48335	Shann ▮▮	Hunt MGB's w/unplugged Gun	R. ▮▮ 3886
C-48336	Curt R. ▮▮	Hunt MGB's w/unplugged Gun	R. ▮▮ 3886
C-48332	Charles ▮▮	Hunt Ducks w/o Fed. Stamp	R. ▮▮ 3886
C-48331	Charles A. ▮▮	Poss. over limit of Ducks	R. ▮▮ 3886
C-48330	Charles A. ▮▮	Take MGB's over bait	R. ▮▮ 3886
C-48329	Thomas J. ▮▮	Hunt Ducks w/o Fed. Stamp	R. ▮▮ 3886
C-48328	Thomas J. ▮▮	Hunt MGB's w/unplugged Gun	R. ▮▮ 3886
C-48327	Thomas J. ▮▮	Poss. over limit of Ducks	R. ▮▮ 3886
C-48326	Thomas J. ▮▮	Take MGB's over bait	R. ▮▮ 3886
C-47747	Rhoddy J. ▮▮	Take MGB's over bait	R. ▮▮ 3886
C-47748	Rhoddy J. ▮▮	Poss. over limit of Ducks	R. ▮▮ 3886
C-47749	Rhoddy J. ▮▮	Hunt MGB's w/unplugged Gun	R. ▮▮ 3886
C-47750	Rhoddy J. ▮▮	Hunt Ducks w/o Fed. Stamp	R. ▮▮ 3886
C-40724	Clifton ▮▮	Hunt MGB's from moving Motorboat	G. Benoit 4329
C-40725	Thomas ▮▮	Hunt MGB's from moving Motorboat	G. Benoit 4329
C-48426	Larry J. ▮▮	Hunt MGB's from moving Motorboat	G. Benoit 4329
C-48327	Brian P. ▮▮	Hunt MGB's from moving Motorboat	G. Benoit 4329
C-48428	David J. ▮▮	Hunt MGB's Illegal Hours	G. Benoit 4329
C-48429	David J. ▮▮	Hunt MGB's w/unplugged Gun	G. Benoit 4329
C-48430	David J. ▮▮	Hunt MGB's w/unsigned Stamp	G. Benoit 4329
C-48432	Oniel J. ▮▮	Hunt MGB's Illegal Hours	G. Benoit 4329

CHARGES FILED BY REGION ___8___

REGIONAL SECRETARY:

HEADQUARTER'S SECRETARY

DATE FILED WITH FEDERAL AUTHORITIES

RECEIVED BY:_____
SIGNATURE

DATE: _____

The media hounded me to make statements. The less I talked, the more the frenzy grew over the document. I was asked if they could use my name. I gave the okay, thinking things could not get much worse.

CHAPTER 14

Bull Red Fish

Tampy T

As destiny would have it, on August 1, 1986, a pilot and I were flying District 8B. I told the pilot to fly where we would not find anyone. We were slowly drifting at three thousand feet. The emerald-green water glistened beneath the wings. There was just a ripple on the water. Everything was peaceful, until I saw a lone boat in the distance circling. I knew it wasn't a trawler.

There was the introduction of the wildly popular dish in New Orleans by Chef Paul Prudhomme, which required millions of pounds of red drum (redfish). Unlike most recipes that utilize smaller fish, this dish did not have a size limit. Some fishermen began to target the larger redfish called bull reds. These fish were usually above twenty-seven inches long up to fifty inches. The impact to the fisheries was that these fish were the spawners. Without these bull redfish, the future of the species was doubtful. According to the biologists, it takes approximately seven years to grow over twenty-seven, or to mature enough to spawn. The bull reds during the months of August and September would congregate in large schools, making them susceptible to slaughter. The laws regulating this fishery were in the infantile phase. The let-them-fish attitude of the politicians and the department was in full force.

The fish could be caught, not by the gills, but with a large seine net, which would encircle the fish. The fish could then be dipped out of the net. The bottom of the net had to remain open, not drawn together forming a large bowl. This allowed some of the fish to escape.

The pilot and I circled the boat to observe the operation. The amazing thing about wildlife is that wildlife can often teach you things that are very significant in life. I began to closely observe these lessons, thus becoming inspired to work harder even under adverse conditions.

The parable of the day was while circling the boat. I observed a large number of bull reds circling inside the net. The fish circled and circled, then as if someone gave them orders, the entire school of fish would target a specific spot in the net, and in unison, the fish would ram the net. No one told the fish to do it, yet they all worked together to achieve a goal—survival.

I was so touched by their efforts, I instructed the pilot to land. I've boarded the sixty-foot-long motor vessel, Tampy T. The captain ignored the fact that I was on the boat. Instead, he was frantically shouting orders to the four-man crew. I asked the captain as he ran around the vessel to estimate the total pounds of fish in the net. He responded, "One hundred thousand pounds." I noticed most fish were caught by the gills in the mesh of the net. The main issue I found were the purse strings on the bottom of the net, which made the net illegal. I observed the captain run past my position and full throttled the huge boat. All of a sudden, the boat began to vibrate and pull sideways. I asked the captain what was happening. He said the fish looked for a weak spot in the net, then the whole school hit that spot to escape. The captain said the fish were often successful in tearing the net and escaping.

I got emotional and ordered the captain to release the fish. The captain warned me that I had better know what I was doing. He stated I was stopping a $20,000-per-hour operation. He resisted, and I said cut the fish loose. About that time, the fish made another attempt to escape. The fish pulled so hard that the net became entangled in the wheel of the vessel. I stayed with the vessel while thousands of pounds of bull reds entangled in the webbing were released overboard. The final attempt by the fish was successful. The fish breached the net.

While in law school, I was told by the dean I should never let emotions, or morality interfere with my decisions. He said laws don't factor in morality. That was why I quit law school. I got the message the fish were sending. My decision was partly based on the law and a moral interpretation, but the main contributing factor to my actions were as much moral as law. All can be accomplished if groups work together.

Apprehensively, I went back to the dock waiting for a backlash of criticism. To my amazement, the department attorney, Spirit of the Law, agreed with my interpretation of the law.

This was another blow to the commercial gill net industry. In fact, after the smoke cleared, my decision resulted in strike three for gill nets. Today, commercial fishing for speckled trout and red drum is nonexistent. The recreational limits on these species are quite limited. Ironically, only one bull red drum may be possessed over twenty-seven inches. This case resulted in the exposure of the industry to slaughter and highlighted monetary profit as the goal rather than maintaining the species.

CHAPTER 15

Lowlife Tactics

The effects of the "epistle," as Secretary Snake-Eyes called it, came to a full boil. The media, GCCA, and the public demanded answers. The federal system was dissecting the allegations with a fine-tooth comb. District Attorney of Terrebonne Parish ordered a full investigation. The everyday pressure of the relentless press took its toll on the chain of command. Frustration led to desperation and revenge. The prophetic bone-chilling threat Secretary Snake-Eyes made on March 24, 1986, stating, "Are you willing to lose everything you have for what you believe in?" came to fruition. The fight became a very personal attack on my family.

My wife and I had been married for twelve years. We had no children. Medical issues affected my wife's ability to get pregnant, and she desperately wanted children. A friend of ours worked for the Louisiana Department of Health and Human Resources as a foster care supervisor. My wife saw this as a way to have children. Although she always wanted one little girl, on June 16, 1982, we received two severely abused boys, ages ten months and two and a half years old. Within six months, we had five special-needs boys. Then we finally got a one-and-a-half-year-old little girl. The Louisiana Plan, as it was called, would limit the time in foster care to one and a half years, then the state would initiate proceedings to terminate parental rights. At this time, we were in the process of adopting the little girl and the first two boys. We had six children in our home at this point. Chaotic, fun, and yet another series of challenges in our lives. Throughout my career, I tried to shield my wife and kids from my hectic life. My wife had to endure women calling, saying they were with me. Phone numbers slipped into my uniform pocket and very disturbing death threats.

On August 5, 1986, Major Boots stated he was going to pick me up to attend a shrimp meeting. The major stated, "I am going to tell you something, Roy, but I don't want you to lose your temper." He said that the department had gone too far with the threats against me, and he didn't want any part of it. This statement made me very nervous. Now they were turning on each other. The major stated, "They are going after your kids. I wouldn't do anything to hurt Sally." He said family is supposed to be off-limits. I asked who initiated this turn of events. The major stated Colonel Ram brought it up to Secretary Snake-Eyes at a recent staff meeting in which the sole purpose was shutting me up. I asked how it would happen. Major Boots said Secretary Snake-Eyes was going to approach secretary of the Department of Health and Human Resources, claiming that I was mentally unstable. He asked me not to tell anyone that he told me of their plans. He said he was sworn to secrecy. The next day, Major Flip and Flop called to disclose the same plans. Major Flip and Flop said that was too dirty to do that to Sally.

This was the most devastating event in my career. I sat and pondered a solution, but my emotions got the best of me. I decided to confront the chief of enforcement. I called him at home late one night and asked him if he was trying to take my kids away. I could tell he was shocked that someone told me. He never denied it. All Colonel Ram kept saying was that the administration was very upset with me. I lost my composure telling the chief to meet me on the road so we could talk about it man-to-man. He said he would not come because I was upset. I told him he was a lowlife coward, and he did not defend himself at all. Instead, his demeanor indicated embarrassment. No apologies were ever offered to Sally or I.

On September 4, 1986, all my agents, except three loyal to me, were summoned to Baton Rouge headquarters. According to the agents, who now had no loyalty to headquarters, the Colonel said I had thirty days left before I would be fired. The agents also said that, allegedly, the colonel told the agents that if some physical harm came to me that the department didn't care.

The colonel had employed a tactic of going to my supporters in an attempt to sway their opinions. This did not work but rather solidified my support. It is my understanding that the colonel scrutinized my cases looking for errors. Part of this tactic allegedly involved the interviewing of violators of all sorts.

On September 6, 1986, the threats of violence became a real reality. My house was situated approximately one hundred feet from a main highway. I had a large front yard where my seven foster kids often played. My wife and I were watching the children when at 3:30 p.m. I heard what I thought was a backfire of a vehicle. The vehicle, an El Camino, was traveling west to east. The same vehicle was now heading from east to west when I heard a distinct blast from a gun that shattered my front door on my house. I told the children to run. My wife, like a mother hen, gathered all the children and ran. This act of violence was the straw that broke the camel's back. This was like a war. How could I defend my family from such acts? I began carrying a gun everywhere I went even while cutting my grass.

Lifetime Subpoena

I decided to call a friend, Dave Hall, of the United States Fish and Wildlife Service. Dave often intervened for me setting the record straight with the uninformed public and irate politicians. Dave Hall called US Attorney John Voltz in New Orleans. Mr. Voltz met with me on September 15, 1986. The meeting consisted of Dave Hall, John Voltz, Bill Mellor, the FBI, and Lance Africk, chief prosecutor. I explained what happened. Mr. Voltz said he had been following me, watching my efforts for quite some time. Mr. Voltz said I was dealing with some very bad people connected to organized crime. He said the shot was a warning. He warned me to be very careful in my everyday life. "Be on the lookout for any suspicious people, or vehicles. Check your car before you get in it." Mr. Voltz then turned to Lance Africk, instructing him to draw up a Federal Grand Jury subpoena with no target. This subpoena, according to Mr. Voltz, would serve as protection from the criminal element I was dealing with. Mr. Voltz said, "If anything happens to you, we will consider the act as tampering with a government witness and pursue the violations." He also instructed me to bring all evidence of corruption to FBI agent D.F. On September 22, 1986, I delivered the cumbersome package to the FBI.

Was the crisis over? No. The health department began to give us the runaround on the adoption process of the little girl, who was now five years old. The state then said we were not able to adopt. The state was going to send the girl to her biological family who were no better than the biological parents. My wife and the little girl were devastated. I decided to push going to the judge handling the case. Even though some of the judges didn't care for me, they felt the state had crossed the line in dealing with these children.

After much backdoor pushing, against the state, we adopted the little girl in April of 1987. The first two little boys we cared for were languishing in a quagmire of incompetent and threatened social workers. Although these two boys were up for adoption the state delayed for years until the biological parents had a girl. The state did not take the little girl away from the same biological parents until after three years when it was discovered that she was sexually molested by her uncle, who was sentenced to prison for the acts.

The adoption papers for these three siblings were lost. The psychologicals were haphazardly prepared. I became bitter toward the system and lashed out. Now we have the whole family of three siblings. It took ten years and a trial to adopt these three children. So much for The Louisiana Plan of eighteen months.

We were able to adopt five children and had custody of two. The adoptions mostly took place during cooperative administrations.

842921

AO 110 (Rev 10/82)

SUBPOENA TO TESTIFY BEFORE GRAND JURY

United States District Court

DISTRICT

TO:

Capt. Roy Chauvin
wherever found

SUBPOENA FOR

☒ Person

☐ Document or Object

YOU ARE HEREBY COMMANDED to appear in the United States District Court at the location, date, and time specified below to testify before the Grand Jury in the above entitled case.

PLACE
500 Camp St.,
Hale Boggs Federal Building
10th Floor
New Orleans, La. 70130

COURTROOM
10th Floor
Rm. 1033

DATE AND TIME

YOU ARE ALSO COMMANDED to bring with you the following document(s) or object(s):[1]

☐ Please see additional information on reverse

This subpoena shall remain in effect until you are granted leave to depart by the court or by an officer acting on behalf of the court.

CLERK
LORETTA G. WHYTE

DATE

(BY) DEPUTY CLERK

This subpoena is issued on application of the United States of America by:

9/15, 1986

NAME, ADDRESS AND PHONE NUMBER OF ASSISTANT U.S. ATTORNEY
Lance Africk
Asst. U.S. Attorney
500 Camp St., Rm. 210
Hale Boggs Fed.Bldg.
New Orleans, La. 70130-

1) If not applicable, enter "none."

99

Diesel Theft

On the same day I met with FBI agent D.F., September 22, 1986, Upon returning home, I was informed by two individuals that they had caught one of my agents stealing diesel at their camp.

This agent had resigned during the Treen Administration and was rehired when the old administration returned as payback to me. The two witnesses gave signed affidavits stating they observed, on September 22, 1986, a marked wildlife boat at their dock. Upon investigation, they found an agent actively taking diesel from their fifty-five-gallon drum. The witnesses stated the agent was in full uniform and ran into the marsh when they confronted him. My investigation was turned over to the department. Due to the political nature of the agents rehiring, the investigation was covered up.

Everyone in the hierarchy of the department became disillusioned. The effects of the "epistle" began to take its toll. Now some wanted to reenter my circle. Let bygones be bygones. I knew that the change in the attitude was due to the fact that the "epistle" was being investigated on several fronts, and they were scared. I did not offer them much relief due to the strategy that if they were worried about themselves they were less likely to get involved in any new conspiracies.

Set Up

I thought the "epistle" would be a death blow to their interference in my job; however, the arrogance of the administration wanting to rub your face in corruption was amazing. On November 20, 1986, Colonel Ram called stating Governor Rico and Secretary Snake-Eyes wanted me to meet Senator Blood Brother at his camp to investigate a claim by Senator BB of an impending set up. It was alleged that someone had put bait out in Senator BB's duck ponds. Major Flip and Flop informed me that Senator BB stated the feds had paid someone to bait his ponds in order to set up Governor Rico. On November 20, 1986, I brought an agent loyal to me as a witness to meet Senator BB at the eight-foot-tall fence he built to keep me out. Senator BB was now overweight, wearing dingy coveralls. He narrowed his entourage to one person. Senator BB put his hand out to shake. I shook his hand. He was very humble, unlike our last meeting in 1976. Senator BB explained his situation to me asking me to go with him to look for bait in his ponds. For three hours, we rode through his ponds searching for bait. Then we went to this huge camp. One could see that it was a party spectacle. I envisioned all the big shots partying.

While at Senator BB's camp, he turned to me asking, "Can I hunt?" I told Senator BB, calmly, that it would have been very nice if I would have been invited to his camp filled with politicians and dignitaries. That could have been fun; however, the condescending attitude toward a lowly agent would have been intolerable. I reminded Senator BB of our battles over the years and asked, "Exactly, what do you want?" Senator BB stated he had been diagnosed with cancer of the throat, the oil industry had failed, and he was broke. He further stated I had prevented him from hunting with Governor Rico at his camp due to the fear of me and the feds. Senator BB stated he did not know how much longer he had to live, but this was a request, not a demand.

As the senator hung his head, I felt sorry for him. The king was defeated, not by me but life. He was abdicating his throne, seeking redemption from the outcast leper. I was touched by his sincerity, but how could I answer him?

I told him, "You can hunt all you want as long as you are legal."

He claimed, "Did you find any bait?"

I said, "No."

Senator BB stated he wanted a letter from me stating there was no bait in his ponds, thus, allowing him and Governor Rico to hunt.

I told Senator BB I did not find bait in his ponds this day, but "what if bait is put out after I leave, or next week, and you have this letter from me?" I told Senator BB this set of circumstances was not fair, asking me to compromise my integrity and ruin my credibility in court. I told Senator BB it was his responsibility to make sure no bait was present during hunting. I said it was also his duty to adhere to all other laws regarding duck hunting. "If you are legal, you can hunt all you want. I will not give you your letter as requested, but I will follow up with a letter to Secretary Snake-Eyes." I sent a scathing letter to Secretary Snake-Eyes informally informing him of all the criminal violations he committed in ordering me to conspire with Senator BB to avoid prosecution by the federal government if caught on a duck violation.

As if they were deaf, on November 24, 1986, four days later, Colonel Ram called and ordered me to go to Senator BB's camp, where he and Governor Rico were hunting to shield them from the feds. I refused to go; however, no threats were made.

During the next few months, the department tried to unravel the "epistle." I began to file federal charges, five years late. All the newly filed charges resulted in convictions with hefty fines. This gave validity to the "epistle," thereby corroborating the illegal activity of my department.

CHAPTER 16

Selective Enforcement

1987 started out with a bang, much like fireworks welcoming a New Year. Resolutions and self-made promises to make the world a better place are usually in order. However, in Louisiana, especially Terrebonne Parish, we seemed to miss out on these dreams. As a department, we were swaddled in unethical and illegal practices, as selective enforcement and good-old-boy tactics prevailed. The current orders from Colonel Ram were to only let two agents, that Senator BB picked, work a specific area around his camp. Agent G and Agent Fish were Senator BB's choices. The specific agents loyal to me were, under no circumstances, allowed in the area according to Colonel Ram. The issue at hand was the hotly debated unattended gill net law. In spite of numerous meetings with the district attorney and the department, the problem continued to exist.

Forbidden Zone

On January 13, 1987, I sent one of my agents into the "forbidden zone" to answer a gill net complaint from the public. The agent observed three subjects taking striped bass (game fish) from a gill net. The agent charged the subjects and asked to see their licenses. One violator stated Agents G. and Fish had checked their licenses earlier. The agent accepted that statement. On January 14, 1987, the agent ran a check of licenses of the entire operation. Checked was the sister of the violator, who owned the boat, nets, and a wholesale seafood business. She was well-connected with the department, especially Colonel Ram. The search for licenses revealed none were purchased for 1987. On the night of January 14, 1987, I sent two agents back to the same area. The agents found four unattended nets filled with game fish. The nets were illegal mesh, and no tags were attached. The agents found the violator miles away sleeping in his boat. He was charged. The violator had no license, just applications, which were not acceptable.

At approximately 3 a.m. on January 15, 1987, the female owner of the operation came to the landing where nets and fish were being off-loaded. She threatened the agents stating Colonel Ram told her she was legal and so had agents G. and Fish. As it turned out, Agents G. and Fish on the same day charged two other fishermen with the same violations that they had let their friends slide being very selective. The owner of the equipment told her brother and others not to sign the citations (which, by signature, is a promise to appear in court), or cooperate with the agents. Her brother and others were arrested and brought to jail. On January 15, 1987, at 10:30 a.m., I was advised by Assistant District Attorney John Walker that the statue required seizure of the vessel. On the same date, Lieutenant Colonel stated the procedure was right; however, he would not give orders to seize the vessel.

At 12:15 p.m. on January 16, 1987, the business owner called demanding her boat registration papers. At 3:45 p.m. on January 16, 1987, I informed the business owner that she would be charged. She stated she did not want agents on her property, and she was calling her lawyer, former acquitted district attorney. She threatened me with Colonel Ram and stated, "You are taking an awful big chance." Accompanying me were three loyal agents and the news media, the CBS affiliate, Channel 4 out of New Orleans. The media had received an anonymous call of a potential violent confrontation. Upon arrival, the owner said she was told by her attorney not to sign the citations, or the boat seizure order.

About this time, a speeding truck filled with men came to the dock, rushing the media and me. The head of the group was the business owner's father, who shouted vulgar threats at me. I told him we were arresting his daughter and him if he did not back off. At this time, one of the agitators lunged at the camera man, trying to throw him and his camera into the canal. The reporter backed his crew off but continued to film. To diffuse the situation, I instructed the agents to handcuff the owner and place her in the back of my car. Tempers continued to flare as we left the parking lot. The twenty-three-foot-long vessel was seized.

On January 23, 1987, Colonel Ram called to say the owner of the vessel changed her mind and would now sign the seizure order. By signing the order, I could release the boat. Colonel Ram said to release the boat. I agreed to release the boat at a neutral site, Sportsman's Paradise, a facility owned by my friend, Stu Scheer.

At 11:30 a.m. on January 24, 1987, I met with the owner of the vessel and her lawyer, who was no friend of Stu Sheer, at Sportsman's Paradise. My friend was to stand by in case of trouble. Immediately, her lawyer became uncooperative and instructed his client not to sign the seizure order. My friend, standing by, noticed I was having trouble with her lawyer, so he took the opportunity to remove the lawyer from his property. My friend gave the attorney thirty seconds to leave his property. The attorney ran toward the highway and stood there, eventually leaving. Colonel Ram called to find out what happened. Colonel Ram said he would talk to the owner again and her lawyer. At 12:00 noon, the owner and lawyer agreed to sign the seizure order clearing the return of the boat.

The Note

On October 15, 1987, I, along with two of my agents, were subpoenaed for the trial of the business owner and her brother. Their defense attorney, formerly acquitted district attorney, subpoenaed the LDWF entourage, including Secretary Snake-Eyes, Colonel Ram, Major Flip and Flop, and Agents Goofy and Bass. After the five-hour trial, Judge Jimmy Gaidry found the defendant guilty on all counts of the unattended net violations, stating the LDWF did not have the authority to interpret laws. That authority rests solely with the trial judge. Judge Gaidry's interpretation of the law was if an agent had to leave the location of the net to find the owner, then the net was considered unattended. This interpretation was in direct conflict with LDWF attorney, Spirit of the Law, who gave numerous interpretations including but not limited to allowing thirty minutes for subjects to arrive. The seafood business owner and her brother entered guilty pleas on license violations, not wanting to expose Colonel Ram's note, stating, "Roxanne, this is your receipt keep until you get your license. Ram."

This note was seized from the business owner when she presented it to me in lieu of an original license, in violation of the law. The note was signed by Colonel Ram.

Louisiana Resident Certification

License No. ______ Tag Nos. 43-49 Date Feb 4, 1986

LOUISIANA DEPARTMENT OF WILDLIFE AND FISHERIES

OFFICE RECEIPT - B. R.

FOR OFFICE USE ONLY

Certified By [illegible]

LICENSE APPLICATION Title [illegible]

NOT A VALID LICENSE Parish or District [illegible]

VOID 45 DAYS

P.O. Box 15570 Baton Rouge, La. 70895

Fee $	$10.00 (50.00 struck out)	1440 4 5 — Class: Gill Net	Name [redacted]
Postage	.25	Type of Net: 55	Street or R.F.D. [redacted]
Total Remittance	10.25 (50.25 struck out)	Parish Code	City or Town [redacted] Parish Terre
Signature of Applicant [redacted]			State La Zip Code 70344
			Telephone Number [redacted]

7	@ 1,200'	na	na	na
No. of Nets	Length of Nets	Vessel Name	Vsl. Length	Vessel Number

* There Will Be A $5.00 Handling Charge On All Returned Checks (N.S.F., Account Closed, Etc.)

Submit this application four to six weeks early to allow sufficient time for your license to be processed and returned to you Prior to beginning operations. **Please apply early. Postage Fee Must Be Included.** Fill out the application completely, including your signature, date and class number. Complete one application for **each** license desired. Do not combine license applications with motor boat registration. Attach the required documentation where requested (ie. vessel COPY affidavit of bill of sale). Remit Personal Check or Cashiers Check only, do not mail cash. Receipts to be used as proof of application can be obtained by presenting this application with required fees to the Baton Rouge or New Orleans License Sections.

It is required to show proof of residency for the initial application of a resident saltwater or freshwater commercial fishing license. Such proof shall be a current Louisiana Drivers License or a voters registration certificate. Application must be certified by the Sheriff's Department, a Wildlife and Fisheries agent or a District Office of the Department of Wildlife and Fisheries.

SEE REVERSE FOR LICENSE CLASS AND DETAILS

DO NOT MAIL CASH

LICENSES - OTHER

License Expires At End Of Season As Prescribed

144001 HUNTING PRESERVE (Expires June 30) 200.00
Public shooting and/or taking of pen-raised game birds.

144002 GAME BREEDER (Expires Dec. 31) 10.00
Raising and selling wild game birds and/or wild game quadrupeds.

144032 NON-GAME QUADRUPED EXHIBITOR (Expires Dec. 31) 10.00
Raising and/or exhibiting non-game quadrupeds.

44033 NON-GAME QUADRUPED BREEDER (Expires Dec. 31) 25.00
Raising, exhibiting and selling non-game quadrupeds.

44007 RESIDENT FUR BUYER (Expires June 30) 25.00
Persons buying, selling and/or shipping raw furs or skins within the state only

44008 RESIDENT FUR [illegible]
Persons or firms [illegible]
shipping out of st[illegible]

44009 NON RESIDENT [illegible]
Non-Resident bu[illegible]
within the state or [illegible]

44010 NON-RESIDENT [illegible]
Non-Residents b[illegible]
ping out of state [illegible]

44046 ALLIGATOR PA[illegible]

44062 RETAIL ALLIGA[illegible]
(Effective Sept. 4

JAN[illegible]

44046 Resident Crab Tra[illegible]

44047 Non-Resident Cra[illegible]

JANUARY 1 - DECEMBER 31

144021 RETAIL DEALER - FISH & SEAFOOD 10.00
A resident buying or selling commercial or bait fish for retail sale to the consumer including oyster counters. Includes retailing shrimp and shucked oysters.

144022 WHOLESALE DEALER 55.00
Residents buying or handling commercial or bait species taken into the state or fresh or processed commercial fish shipped into the state for sale to wholesale or retail dealers or to ship out-of-state. Includes any person, firm or corporation taking commercial fish and shipping or transporting such fish beyond the state.

144023 WHOLESALE DEALER'S AGENT 15.00
Persons purchasing for wholesale dealer.

[illegible] NON-RESIDENT RETAIL DEALER - FISH & SEAFOOD ... 55.00
[illegible]mercial or bait fish for [illegible]ster counters. Includes

[illegible]LER 155.00
[illegible]ommercial fish or bait [illegible] processed commercial [illegible] to wholesale or retail [illegible]sh out of the state.

[illegible]ORT 205.00
[illegible]imp, or oysters, unless [illegible] or hauling own catch [illegible] of wholesale dealer's

[illegible] 205.00
[illegible]ows wholesale in the

[illegible] 15.00
[illegible] sale including frogs,

Ro[redacted]
This is your receipt
keep until you get your
lic.
Ray

STATE OF LOUISIANA   CITY COURT OF HOUMA
VS. NO. 8601998-01 thru -08   PARISH OF TERREBONNE
████████████   STATE OF LOUISIANA

STATE OF LOUISIANA
VS. NO. 8601997-01 thru -03
████████████

REASONS FOR NOLLE PROSEQUI

The State will enter a Nolle Prosequi on all charges based on: the sworn testimony of Wildlife & Fisheries agents ████████████ and ████████████ in the trial of Joseph Billiot 8601440-01 thru -11 which testimony indicated that Ray Montet, Chief Enforcement officer of Wildlife & Fisheries Department, authorized the defendants to fish the gill nets in question in the manner for which they were cited; that defendants were fishing nets belonging to ████████████; that ████████, through special consent and permission assisted ████████████ in obtaining licenses and tags for the nets in question although the same licenses and tags were not available to the general public.

The State disagrees with the position of Wildlife & Fisheries on its interpretation of "unattended" nets especially in light of past meetings between the Terrebonne Parish District Attorney's office, Wildlife & Fisheries agents, Colonel ████████ and Major ████████. The State was at no time advised that Wildlife & Fisheries had changed its position to one contrary to that of the Terrebonne Parish District Attorney's office said position having been previously expressed in writing to the Wildlife & Fisheries .

Based on the above reasons the State cannot in good faith prosecute these cases although it feels legitimate violations occurred since the ranking enforcement official of Wildlife & Fisheries authorized the cited conduct contrary to the position of the Terrebonne District Attorney's office.

John R. Walker
JOHN R. WALKER ASSISTANT DISTRICT

December 1, 1986

Captain Roy Chauvin
Route 1, Box 5241
Gibson, Louisiana 70356

Secretary Department of Wildlife and Fisheries
7389 Florida Boulevard
Baton Rouge, Louisiana 70806

Dear Mr. ████████,

I am in receipt of your letter dated October 30, 1986, (exhibit 1)
which, as I understand is the results of your investigation as the
same relates to the Grievance Hearing which I requested. At this
hearing, which was openly tape recorded by your staff and I separately
on October 9, 1986 in the presence of Mrs. ██████████ Personnel
officer, Mr. ██████████████, Attorney for the Department, and you,
as the hearing officer, I specifically requested that my four-page
letter to Major ████████ dated June 25, 1986 be answered in its
entirety (exhibit 2). This request was the total basis of my
grievance because I did not understand the remarks on my Satisfactory
Civil Service rating. The importance of my understanding the remarks
is predicated by the fact that Mrs. ████ stated that these remarks
could be used in future ratings if it is determined that the alleged
problem is on-going. Furthermore, Major ████████ threatened that if
I did not accept this rating that I would receive another rating
similar to this one. This violates the intent of the Grievance
Process. I am as confused as ever with these remarks on my rating
and once again request that my four page letter cited above be
answered in its entirety to clarify the ambiguities which could
be deduced from such broad and derogatory statements.

Your findings of October 30, 1986 are very unfair because I was
not afforded the opportunity to address some of the statements,
which is the new basis of your allegations. Had these statements
been divulged at the hearing on October 9, 1986 I would possibly
not have had to respond as I am now. In addition, your findings
raise new questions as the same relate to the letter of October 30,
1986. In each step of the grievance I have been given different
answers to the same questions as is evident in Major ████████
initial answer to to the four page letter of June 25, 1986. In
Major ████████ July 2, 1986 response(exhibit 3) there was no
evidence to corroborate any of the allegations. However, in
his personal meeting with you Major ████████ has changed his basis
for the rating. This is very confusing to say the least.

All I am requesting is straight-forward answers not filled with suppositions and inuendoes, but fact. Once again I would like to object to the non-compliance of the specific rules governing the Grievance Procedure Policy of the Louisiana Department of Wildlife and Fisheries as the same related to time limitations and the investigative process etc. in each step of my grievance.

In point one of your letter of October 30, 1986 Major ████████ stated to you "...you want complete control of your district without regard to procedures set forth by the Enforcement Division."etc.

1. How have my actions exhibited that I want complete control of District 8B?

2. What do you specifically mean when you say that I want complete control of District 8B?

3. What procedures of the Enforcement Division have I not followed?

4. How has District 8B operated differently from the other districts throughout the state?

Please give specific examples of any and all evidence to support your allegations. Please furnish me with copies of the written procedures of the Enforcement Division as the same relate to my duties, in which you are alleging I have disregarded.

Major ████████s specific example to corroborate point one is very misleading and innacurate. Major ████████ was fully aware of the fact that I had been storing seized equipment at my residence for quite some time prior to this rating. Major ████████ was informed that I was under a court order to store seized nets at my residence. This court order was issued by City Court Judge Jude Fanguy. I informed Judge Fanguy of my orders from the Department which resulted in Judge Fanguy's court order to you dated September 26, 1985(exhibit 4). I did comply with the orders of the Department, in spite of a court order to the contrary, and all of the nets are stored at the warehouse on Horde Street in Harahan, Louisiana.

This fact poses several questions:

1. Does a court order take precedent over Department policy?

2. Could I be held in contempt of a court order for not obeying the orders of the court?

3. Should I release equipment to violators if I receive a court order from Judge Fanguy or from any judge with competent jurisdiction over said matters?

The irony to this example is that for years former District Attorney ████████ held all guns that were seized by the Department. There was no objection from the Department to this policy. Major ████████ was aware of this policy with ████████, but he did not object either.

111

Also certain pieces of evidence are not being stored at the warehouse in Harahan, allegedly for lack of space and/or facilities. I am currently running my personal freezer at my expense to hold perishable evidence for the Department which is needed in court. Furthermore, I am and have been in possession of numerous boats, motors, trailers,etc. which are and were being stored at my residence.(exhibit 5). In all cases we were ordered to seize the equipment. At present we are in possession of the ████ ████ boat and another boat belonging to ████████ stored at personal residences for lack of facilities, but ordered to seize.

The discrepancies in policy are quite obvious and discriminatory in nature. I would ask that you please clarify, in writing, the Department's positions as the same relates to the storage of seized equipment at personal residences. I am not asking for restitution in the out-of-pocket expenditures, but a little justice as the same relates to evidence problems.

Also in conjunction with the statement concerning the goals of the Enforcement Division I am confused as to what are the specific goals. Statistically, in quantity and most important quality, District 8B has led the entire state for the past five years in enforcement work, according to enforcement records. The stats are staggering and out of balance with respect to the rest of the state. All of the Agents in District 8B are consistently showing up in the Top 20 Agents in the state each month. District 8B has been criticized for overshadowing other districts. This consistent effort could not be accomplished without hard, dedicated teamwork.

A typical example of the criticism was in the bass case on March 9,1983 where 2 subjects in the U.S.Bass Tournament fraudulently won the $1,000 top prize. Both subjects received stiff penalties for the crime and the case got nation-wide attention. Agents participating in the case worked long arduous hours. There were no news releases from the Department, however, I was ordered to write a statement as to why I was in another Region and whether or not I had tried to contact the supervisors and agents of Region 6 before I made the case. This chain of events was very unfair.

In point two of your investigation I felt that the evidence, copies of which you have, that I presented at the hearing far outweighed the claims of Major ████████. I supplied you with a list of several hundred phone calls which I responded to in a very short period of time. In addition, I supplied you with a statement signed by District 8B Agents stating that they had no problems in getting in touch with me.

Once again new answers have surfaced relative to my availability and this time I think that this was done in poor taste. I do not think that my wife should have been used in the statement, nor was I presented with these allegations at the hearing. Upon receipt of this statement I asked my wife if she had ever told Major ████████ that I was sleeping or in the crawfish pond during this rating period. My wife replied, "No".

I feel that these actions are a desperate attempt to justify the rating. I have seven foster children under the age of twelve years and it is quite impossible to sleep after day light at my house no matter how late I work. Also my six acre crawfish pond in my back yard has not been flooded nor worked for the past two years. Major ████████ claims are totally inaccurate and misleading.

Since I have been Captain I have spent hundreds of dollars which were never reimbursed by the Department, out of my own pocket on long distant phone calls in order to do my job efficiently. I am not bringing this fact up facetiously, but I feel that there is no basis whatsoever for any statements in point 2. I take exception to the biased and unfair statements about my wife's credibility as alleged in point 2. I will continue to field all phone calls and I am in the market for a phone-answering device which will serve as a record of calls for future reference.

Mr. ██████, point 3 is the heart of the rating, which received a great deal of attention at all steps of the hearing process, but once again a direct allegation is not supported with corroborative evidence. I do not want to be redundant, but I am totally baffled by the allegation. These assumptions misrepresent the facts and once again these allegations raise serious questions which no one will answer. I would ask that you specifically enumerate the guidelines that you are alleging were set forth by the City Court Judge and the D.A.'s office that I followed in lieu of the procedures set forth by the Department of Wildlife and Fisheries.

In order to move forward and to set the record straight I will have to enumerate the events which have formed the basis of the remarks on my rating. I can only ascertain that you are referring to four major events which occurred during my rating period causing a great deal of confusion. In chronological order the following events occurred:

1. Enforcement of the unattended net law.

2. Boat seizures in Terrebonne Parish.

3. Enforcement of the inside-outside shrimp line at Caminada Pass.

4. Senator ████████████'s working relationship with me, as the same relates to my job.

In early Spring of 1985 Major ██████ was receiving a number of complaints on unattended nets. The nets were an eye-sore to the sports and other commercial netters alike. After my request on how he wanted the law enforced, Major ██████ first instructions were that the Department's unofficial position was to pick up unattended gill nets only if we had to. I was ordered to pick up an unattended net every now and then only to please the sports. This method did not work and the complaints continued to mount.

113

Major ████ said the Department's position changed again. Now we were ordered to pick up nets that were left unattended for 3 to 4 hours. Major ████ was subsequently criticized in a newspaper article by Bob Marshall, according to Major ████. Then our orders changed to say if the man is in the vicinity of the net do not pick it up ████ Case exhibit 6). Then our orders changed to say if the nets were left out over night then pick it up. The orders changed again and we were instructed not to pick up unattended nets unless there were dead fish in the same. I continually asked for concise orders concerning gill nets and the official position be handed down from the appropriate authority to put an end to the confusion.

On September 26, 1985 A.D.A. John Walker, in behalf of D.A. Doug Greenburg, requested a meeting to discuss policies and procedures. (exhibit 7) On October 9, 1985 I received a copy of a letter from you addressed to John Walker in reference to a meeting, but it was your decision that I would not be invited to the meeting, even though I requested the same in writing.(exhibit 8) Shortly thereafter a meeting did take place, however. I was never notified of the results through the chain of command as indicated.

Then on December 16, 1985 there was a meeting in Houma, Louisiana at Mr. Greenburg's office. In attendance were some of the Agents of District 3B, Colonel ████, Major ████, Mr. Greenburg, John Walker and I. The issue of unattended nets came up and Colonel ████ stated that he could not speak for the Department, but policy changed from day to day and it was impossible for Colonel ████ to give definite guidelines on how to enforce the law. Enforcement was left up to the discretion of the Agent.

On January 17, 1986, in a letter addressed to you(exhibit 9) Mr. Greenburg asked for policies and positions of the Department with respect to unattended gill nets. Mr. Greenburg felt that 15 minutes was long enough to establish whether or not a net was unattended. At this time our orders were to give the fishermen a break if they were "half-ass" trying. On February 25, 1986 in a letter(exhibit 10) addressed to Mr. Greenburg from you official policy was written concerning unattended nets. We were ordered to enforce "the spirit and intent of the statute," which is as confusing as ever. This official position encompasses all of the different interpretations above.

Mr. ████ in each different phase of our enforcement of unattended nets I honestly tried to comply with the orders, but in fact I could never comply because the orders kept changing. These orders did not come from outside the Department, they came from my supervisors. I followed the guidelines of the Department on a day to day basis as best as possible.as the same relate to unattended nets. It is Colonel ████s statement that definite guidelines were impossible however, I am being unjustly criticized for not following the specific guidelines of the Department which do not exist. Please cite any and all examples in which I did not follow the guidelines and suggestions of the Department.

The second problem was that of the boat seizures in Terrebonne Parish. The overall Department stand was not to seize boats, except in a deer or shocking fish violation. The position of Mr. Greenburg was to enforce the letter of the law...shall seize boats. On or about April 22, 1985 Lt. Col. ████████'s instructions relative to boat seizures were "go by the law... Burt wants you to go by the law." I don't know who told Mr. Greenburg what, but he was under the impression that we were going to seize boats. On May 3, 1985 in a closed-season shrimp violation involving the boat "Lady Shelley" I was ordered not to take the boat. I complied with those orders. I did not take the boat "Lady Shelley" on May 3, 1985. However, on May 4, 1985 my orders changed and I was ordered to seize the boat "Lady Shelley".

Orders remained inconsistent and confusing. In a letter to Major ████████ on September 22, 1985(exhibit 11) I again complied with orders not to seize a boat belonging to ████████. Also I asked for my orders concerning boat seizures in writing and requested a meeting to resolve the problem. To this date my orders are not to not to seize a boat unless I contact Major ████████ first. Also I am instructed not to seize boats that are in violation but in close proximity to the inside-outside shrimp line. Also I am ordered not to seize shrimp boats that are pulling a test trawl during the closed season. Major ████████ told me that the written orders of February 25, 1986 were to appease Doug Greenburg only and not to be strictly followed in other areas of District 8B nor Region 8. These orders contradict those orders in your letter to Mr. Greenburg of February 25, 1986 relative to seizures, Due to the remarks on my rating, I will assume Major ████████'s orders are recent interpretations of official policy and I will continue to comply with the same until such time my orders change.

1. Please clarify the current official position on boat seizure policy.

2. Please cite any and all examples where I did not comply with the suggestions and guidelines of the Department relative to boat seizures.

3. Please cite any and all examples where I chose to follow the guidelines set forth by the City Court Judge and the D.A.'s office rather than procedures set forth by the Department of Wildlife and Fisheries relative to boat seizures.

Also during my rating period the enforcement of the shrimp line at Caminada Pass in Jefferson Parish caused a great deal of confusion. At a pre-trial conference in Jefferson Parish in October of 1984 before Judges ████████ and ████████, I was chastised by Judge ████████ for not allowing fishermen to butterfly to the powerlines during the closed season. The powerlines were clearly inside the inside-outside shrimp line. I was ordered to quote the legal line to the fishermen at meetings, but in fact I was ordered by the Department "off the record", to give fishermen to the powerlines.

I asked for these orders in writing, but I was refused the same. On August 7, 1985 I was ordered to stay out of Caminada Pass and told that I was no longer in charge of the area. The reason given was that I had instructed Agent ███████████ to enforce the law at Caminada Pass. After two years of harassment, numerous threats, and court appearances the orders were changed by House Bill 1676 which amended the Inside-outside shrimp line relative to Caminada Pass to read "...to the powerlines..."

I never did receive any of the orders concerning Caminada Pass in writing and neither did any of the agents of District 8B, who requested the same in writing. Those orders were very confusing and unfair to the agents involved. There were changes in the verbal wording of the orders from agent to agent and time to time. The public nor the agents knew what line was being enforced. I feel that I was unfairly removed from my enforcement duties at Caminada and I contend that my removal was politically motivated.

The last problem is one that is on-going. This deals with my working relationship with politicians within District 8B, especially Senator ███████████. At the hearing of October 9, 1986 I asked that inside and outside parties be enumerated. Please correct me if I am wrong, but as I understanding this rating City Court Judge Jude Fanguy and District Attorney Douglas Greenburg are outside parties.

City Court Judge Jude Fanguy has never offered any suggestions to me whatsoever concerning the policies of the Department. The paradox to this allegation is that policy was dictated by District Judge ███████ as the same related to Wildlife and Fisheries policy concerning shrimp enforcement at Caminada Pass. Therefore, I am assuming that Judge ███████ is not an outside party. Likewise, District Attorney Douglas Greenburg has not offered any suggestions or guidelines to me other than to "do your job". Mr. Greenburg's suggestions and guidelines were made to you and written policy from you followed as is documented. I have tried to follow the guidelines and suggestions of the Department, but they are very confusing at times. Mr. ███████ stated that it was not fair for an Agent to guess at what his orders were. Mr. ███████ also encouraged the questioning of orders in writing so that clear guidelines could be established. Mr. ███████ cited the diverse opinions within the Department with respect to the bull redfish seine case. In this case Mr. ███████ stated that Major ███████ and I had made the right decision. The confusing nature of many orders has caused me to follow Mr. ███████ recommendation.

Mr. ███████, I specifically asked you at the hearing what part should politics and politicians play in my day to day decisions as the same relate to my duties as a first line supervisor in the Enforcement Division. I explained that I did understand the political system but I only asked that I not be used as a pawn in the system because this action inhibited my ability to do my job honestly and fairly across the board.

Throughout the rating I was told that politics did play a role in my job. I am totally confused to what extent and what politicians. Please clarify the political aspects of my job as the same relates to my duties as an Enforcement Captain within the guidelines and suggestions of the Department of Wildlife and Fisheries. I have been unfairly criticized by the remarks on this rating and I contend that the basis for the same stems from a political situation over-which I have no control. I feel that politics should not have been a major contributing factor for the remarks on the rating.

To qualify these statements, I was told by Major ██████, in his answer to me verbally concerning this rating that politics was a definite factor used to put me in my place. I was told by ██████ that he could not control Senator ██████s influence over you and that a great deal of my problem with the Department was "down the bayou" with Senator ██████. Major ██████ stated that he could not protect me anymore from my non-political stand and suggested that I quit. Major ██████ also stated that I would never get along with the Department and this administration unless I followed your orders at our March 24, 1986 meeting in which you ordered me to offset the G.C.C.A. Petition with a letter addressed to President Cornell Arceneaux stating there was no political influence or pressure in my job. I was threatened with removal from my position if I did not write the statement. This order resulted in the 270-plus page document citing specific examples of political pressure and influence from parties inside and outside of the Department. To substantiate this, the most significant factor in my rating was that I was told by Major ██████ that District Attorney Doug Greenburg was after the ██████ Administration and Senator ██████ and that Doug Greenburg was using me to get at his political enemies and I was going to suffer because of this. I was told that I could go to work for Doug Greenburg after I lost my job with the Department. I was told by Major ██████ that I was in "cahoots" with Dave Hall of the U.S. Fish and Wildlife Service and the Federal Government to make the Department look bad. I have continually been chastised for my working relation-ship with the Federal Goverment and I was also told by Major ██████ that our orders were not to work a Federal Case, because of this allegation. Mr. ██████, I am not involved in a conspiracy with Dave Hall, or anyone., Dave Hall and all of the Agents of the U.S. Fish & Service have enjoyed a very good working relationship with all of the agents of District 8B. We have a relationship which is above board and without petty jealousies. Our recent corporation cases have gained a great deal of respect and exhibit a working relation-ship which is exemplary. Dave Hall has never offered any suggestions to me which would indicate that the Federal Government was involved in a conspiracy to discredit the Department of Wildlife and Fisheries. These allegations are unfounded and I would ask that the Department's position be clarified with respect to working with the Agents of the U.S. Fish and Wildlife Service. To avoid confusion I would ask that the same be specific and placed in writing.

Mr. ████████ I know that all of the above is the reason for the remarks on my rating. I feel that these remarks on my rating are an integral part of the suffering Major ████████ was referring to earlier. I feel threatened and intimidated by the events which have taken place, especially by the investigative process which has not been objective at all. I have been approached by Agents and the public with various claims of possible misconduct in the investigative process, including, but not limited to threats of transfer in positions, physical violence condoned by the Department, solicitation of statements, and my relationship with my seven foster children. Also, for the first time in twelve years, an act of physical violence to my property, endangering the lives of my family. On September 6, 1986 a single blast from a shotgun or rifle shattered my front door during daylight hours. The subjects have returned twice since the incident. I feel that this act was very coincidental, in light of the recent statements such as "You are going to suffer." We are going to put you in your place. You are going to have to be defensive.

Also in conjunction with my working relationship with the Federal Government, I was placed in a very delicate position with respect to my orders on November 20, 1986 to meet with Senator ████████ ████████ on November 21, 1986 at his duck lease because it was alleged that he had been "set up" with bait in his duck ponds and the season was to open on November 22,1986. I was specifically ordered to go into everyone of Senator ████████'s duck ponds with Senator ████████ to look for bait and if I found bait I was to warn Senator ████████ about the violation. These orders set a very serious precedent because this action will come back to haunt me in future court appearances especially in the case involving ████████ ████████ and ████████. This policy discriminates against the hundreds of people who have been cited for hunting over baited ponds and have not had the priviledge of being warned.

Senator ████████ was very cordial, unlike past encounters, but he told me that he received a call from an employee of the Department of Wildlife and Fisheries stating that he had been set up. Senator ████████ told me that the Governor and others were supposed to hunt with him on opening day, but all of that was ruined with the alleged set up.

Mr. ████████ there were implications made that I had something to do with the set up and there was a statement made that the Feds paid someone to bait the ponds to get at the Governor. These are very serious allegations, but the same were substantiated by the fact that I was personally ordered to supervise the detail and give the results of my investigation to Colonel ████████, followed by a verbal O.K. to hunt the ponds.

For the record, I did not find any bait on November 21, 1986, however, that does not mean that bait was not present on or before November 22, 1986. Nor does it mean that bait is not present now or will be present in the future.

I feel as though I was set up to effectively eradicate any possible pending federal investigation concerning the alleged violations on Senator ███████ duck lease. Also, for the record, I have never, nor will I ever, work a baiting case where facts substantiate that the individual was set up. Also, for the record, I will never warn anyone of an impending investigation and I will enforce the law indiscriminately. Please clarify the Policies and Positions of this Department with respect to Federal Migratory Game Bird baiting violations.

I feel that these allegations have dealt a very serious and unfair blow to my integrity as a professional conservation law enforcement officer, for my only goal is to find justice for wildlife and the good people we are to serve. Once again I am not satisfied with the remarks in my satisfactory rating, nor am I satisfied with the results of the Grievance Hearing in the letter of October 30, 1986. I wish to know what is the next step that I may take within the guidelines of the Department of Wildlife and Fisheries and the Department of Civil Service in which to address these allegations.

Captain Roy Chauvin
Supervisor of Enforcement District 8B
Louisiana Department of Wildlife and Fisheries
Terrebonne and Lafourche Parishes

Captain Roy Chauvin 2758

xc: ███████████, Attorney Department Wildlife and Fisheries.
    ███████, Personnel Officer Department of Wildlife and Fisheries
    Herbert Sumrall, Director of State Civil Service.

The following is the attached list of exhibits:

Exhibit One--Letter of October 30, 1986.
Exhibit Two--Letter of June 25, 1986.
Exhibit Three--Letter of July 2, 1986.
Exhibit Four--Letter of September 26, 1985.
Exhibit Five--Letter of May 26, 1983.
Exhibit Six--Letter of February 20,1986.
Exhibit Seven--Letter of September 26, 1985.
Exhibit Eight--Letter of October 9, 1985.
Exhibit Nine--Letter of January 17,1986.
Exhibit Ten--Letter of February 25, 1986.
Exhibit Eleven--Letter of September 22, 1985.

CHAPTER 17

Agent Versus Agent

1987 was quite a different year. My stand with the "epistle" rallied forces behind me, thus, resulting in the GCCA petition creating a frenzy of meetings and irrational decisions. The media would not let the issues die. There would be a lull in the action, as if taking a deep breath, then resurrecting the issues again and again and again. This frustration was compounded by a grand jury subpoena with my name, no case listed. It was as if US Attorney John Voltz sent a blank subpoena challenging all that threatened me, projecting the question: Who wants to be first? We will just fill in the blanks.

I don't know for a fact, but due to the lack of open attacks on me, or threats, I felt certain this subpoena was circulated from Governor Rico on down. They were smart enough to find the hidden message that the subpoena rang out loud to the point they were foaming at the mouth, like a rabid dog, just looking for someone to bite. They decided to fight each other if they could not bite me openly.

A series of clandestine meetings took place with politicians and agents. During this time, I presented an analogy to Major Flip and Flop. I told him the department had taken me on like a hired gun in an Old Western tale. The two gunfighters, the department and me, squared off in the street with loaded guns. The department gunfighter hastily shot all its bullets at one time missing the other gunfighter. The other gunfighter walks up to the smoking gun, which is empty, as the department gunfighter pleas for mercy. The other gun-fighter holsters his loaded gun for another day, leaving the LDWF gunfighter pondering, *How many more bullets does this gun fighter have ready?*

Treasonous Years

A new tactic was born inside the department's self-serving walls. Anyone, within the department, who thought they could take me down silently, would be rewarded with a promotion. On March 4, 1987, Major Inspector Boots stated Colonel Ram was promised the deputy secretary position within the LDWF. The dirty dealings with one another were being revealed to me because of unkept promises to get rid of me. I did not believe the sincerity of these treason-ous agents. Unlike me, who wanted justice, they wanted revenge. I played along with their games for informational purposes. It also served me well to have them fight with one another, losing sight of me. My grandmother had a saying, "Listen to all you hear but never say all you know." Therefore, my ears were wide open and my mouth shut during these meetings with the counterintelligence agenda. In retrospect, the secret meeting on February 13, 1986, was revealed to me by disgruntled agents. The meeting consisted of those agents sometimes loyal to the department, Secretary Snake-Eyes, Colonel Ram, Major Inspector Boots, Major Flip and Flop, and Lieutenant Colonel Cook, whose job it was to tape the meeting and deliver the same to Senator Blood Brother.

Disgruntled Agents Treason

I was not invited to the meeting, nor my three loyal agents. Those agents attending the meeting were instructed not to place the meeting on their time sheets in order to avoid my knowledge of such a meeting. The meeting was supposed to be a blindsided endeavor; however, "the best laid plans of mice and men often go astray," espe-cially if there is a big cat ready to eat the mouse. The participants of the meeting were all alike—looking to benefit at my cost. Sticking to the truth was impossible for this group, so an even-darker side of agents was hatched at this meeting, which was nothing less than a conspiracy to hurt me and my family. One treasonous agent revealed the entire contents of the meeting to me after not being promoted to lieutenant, which was promised by Colonel Ram. It was a major concern, according to the agent, to defuse the sting of the GCCA petition. This agent went to a number of GCCA members and unsuccessfully attempted to derail the petition. The agent said he only made enemies with the public.

According to this agent, at the meeting each agent had a turn to blast me, but none offered a viable solution. As a precursor to our problem to adopt our children, the agent disclosed the original plot to take the children away. Agent G allegedly informed the group I had a nervous breakdown when I first graduated from college. Agent G further stated that the breakdown was so serious that I had to see a psychiatrist. It is difficult to defend a lie. Discussion at the meeting was an attempt to hold a sanity hearing on me within the Department of Health and Human Resources that's the potential reason for psychological exams prior to adoption. I attended at least one exam that seemed to be misplaced by the Department of Health. The plot and method to take away our children had unfolded. There was also discussion that we took in foster children only for the money. This was how low the agents and department stooped.

On March 20, 1987, all the agents began to heat up the fighting with one another. Colonel Ram had a meeting to quell the now-uncontrollable agents who realized they had been lied to. The department had always put a time limit on my disposal, usually thirty days, while years had passed, and I was still there. Also on March 20, 1987, Colonel Ram and Major Flip and Flop called me into a meeting. The hypocrite Colonel stated, "Let's start over. Tell me what you want." I referred to the quote "Listen to all you hear." On April 6, 1987, Major Flip and Flop said the Colonel pressured him to fabricate a lie about me. The department was looking for an independent investigator to follow me. I caught their investigator with binoculars in a tree behind my house. After the discovery, the investigator never came back.

My informant agent did not receive his promotion as promised. Instead, the promotion was given to his archenemy, who had jumped the gun with his own tape recorder and played the same for Senator BB. My informant sought vengeance through me. Everybody was taping each other from the headquarters staff to the field agents, so much so that I heard there was a short supply of tape recorders at local vendors. Have to laugh sometimes. It was ultimately decided by Secretary Snake-Eyes and Colonel Ram that Major Flip and Flop had to be replaced. Major Inspector Boots would take over District 8B. Only Major Inspector Boots was promised the Lieutenant Colonel's position if he succeeded in getting my job. Major Flip and Flop, who informed me of this plot, was very upset. He also became an informant feeding me illegal activities of those in headquarters, not for justice but once again for vengeance. One example was an unpaid four-thousand-acre hunting lease acquired in exchange for guaranteed patrols by enforcement authorities in headquarters.

Then Dave Hall of the US Fish and Wildlife Service jammed up Secretary Snake-Eyes in a request to allow a Japanese film crew to follow me on patrol. A Japanese film crew from Osaka, Japan, wanted to observe my lifestyle for seven days. Secretary Snake-Eyes caved into Dave Hall's request. I was to have free rein on the assignment. The problem that Secretary Snake-Eyes ran into was he was too embarrassed to inform the chain of command of my assignment. When questioned by the chain of command about my whereabouts, I volunteered nothing, placing Secretary Snake-Eyes in the frying pan. I told the staff to call Secretary Snake-Eyes. Now, it appeared Secretary Snake-Eyes had cut their throats as well on my behalf.

On May 11, 1987, Major Flip and Flop informed me he was tired of fighting. His reason was he felt Secretary Snake-Eyes, Colonel Ram, and Major Inspector Boots had betrayed him.

On May 13, 1987, at a district 8B meeting in Thibodaux, Louisiana, Secretary Snake-Eyes started saying things had to change in District 8B. Also in attendance was Colonel Ram, Major Inspector Boots, and Major Flip and Flop. This time, the agents loyal to me were not excluded. My agent, Gary Benoit, interrupted the meeting asking Secretary Snake-Eyes why he wasn't invited to the secret meeting in Baton Rouge on February 13, 1986.

Secretary Snake-Eyes stated, "You didn't ask."

Agent Benoit countered stating, "You did not want me there because I support Roy."

Agent Benoit became very emotional. Agent Benoit said one disloyal agent taped two agents loyal to Roy talking about Senator BB. This disloyal agent took pictures of the two agents and the tape to Senator BB. The colonel and secretary said the problem was Roy.

Colonel Ram asked agent Benoit if he had called everybody at headquarters crooks. Agent Benoit said, "Yes, I don't trust anybody but Roy." Secretary explained he was trying to keep District 8B split for support.

On May 13, 1987, according to reliable sources, Secretary Snake-Eyes, Colonel Ram, district attorney of Terrebonne Parish, and Assistant DA John Walker had a meeting to discuss the Colonel's allegation that I was working for the district attorney. The infuriated district attorney who turned the table on the secretary and colonel by asking if they knew about the investigation on agent over a diesel theft. The DA stated that he could not pursue charges because someone got to the witnesses, who decided not to file charges.

As the wheels of disloyalty turned, Major Flip and Flop informed me that Secretary Snake-Eyes was tired of the colonel's rhetoric. Secretary Snake-Eyes told Major Flip and Flop that I would get Colonel Ram before Colonel Ram gets me. Secretary Snake-Eyes asked Major Flip and Flop who continued to stir up trouble with Senator BB. The Major allegedly said that Agent G had a big mouth. According to Major Flip and Flop, Secretary Snake-Eyes seemed to be confused, saying he thought Agent G was loyal to them. Major Flip and Flop said, "How do you think Roy would find out about everything at the secret meetings?" The major said Agent G had a big mouth that would get everyone in trouble.

The major told Secretary Snake-Eyes, "If you take out any of Roy's agents, he will take out your agents."

Secretary Snake-Eyes asked, "What does Roy have on them?"

Major Flip and Flop told secretary Snake-Eyes he didn't know, but Major Flip and Fop said, "I know Roy well enough that he won't lie down and take it."

According to Major Flip and Flop, Secretary Snake-Eyes then turned on him saying he was not doing his job to control me. Major Flip and Flop said Agent G was the big problem. Secretary Snake-Eyes told Major Flip and Flop that it sounded like Colonel Ram was a problem too. Major Flip and Flop said he was taken off the list of witnesses in the Sevin case because he told the department he would tell the truth.

The Major had predicted I would give Agent G a bad civil service rating due to his activities over the past year. Major Flip and Flop informed me he told Secretary Snake-Eyes, "Here comes Roy. You might lose one of your agents."

On May 22, 1987, an unusual source called Captain CC of the Terrebonne Parish sheriff's office. Captain CC said the sheriff wanted him to meet with Secretary Snake-Eyes and Colonel Ram. The department, according to Captain CC, disguised the meeting to look like the department was looking into the diesel theft. The meeting quickly turned on me, Captain CC said. Captain CC said Roy kept to himself, not involving the sheriff in his dealings, which the sheriff liked. Captain CC said he never really worked with me and never had any problems. The department was still grasping at straws to get rid of me. After the meeting, Captain CC said the agent had called him about the diesel investigation. The agent told Captain CC he was covering his tracks because I had set him up in the diesel theft. Later, according to Captain CC, he saw the agent at the acquitted DA's office. Captain CC said one of the victims/witnesses was there as well, allegedly giving a different statement that contradicted the witness's earlier statement to me. According to Captain CC, the new statement was secret and not to get out. The fix was on and nothing ever came as a result of the investigation. I suppose an eyewitness account of the crime was not enough. Justice for all.

On May 27, 1987, Major Flip and Flop was totally frustrated by the statement he was not doing his job. Major Flip and Flop found out about a not-so-secret meeting to replace him. Secretary Snake-Eyes, under the table, exposed the contents of the meeting.

On May 30 1987, which I dubbed as "confession week," the agent, who received his promotion from Senator BB in exchange for not being loyal to me, decided he no longer needed the department. Deep down, he feared my perseverance. Even though he was promoted, he was still my subordinate. This agent disclosed the contents of a secret meeting on March 11, 1987. In attendance was Secretary Snake-Eyes, Colonel Ram, the agent, and others. According to the promoted agent, Senator BB pounded his fist on the desk, shouting at Secretary Snake-Eyes, "Roy is still here!"

Then on June 8, 1987, Colonel Ram called me to find out who told about the March 11 Senator BB meeting. Really, unlike them, I kept my mouth shut. The department felt I was spying on them with a sophisticated network of informants. The department had created this monster of miscreants who had no loyalty. The frustration now became paranoia. The colonel stated we were still friends and wanted to talk. The colonel talked to a deaf ear.

Now, everyone wanted to jump on the bandwagon needing my help to expose corruption in their individual areas. One interesting bit of information came from region seven, which encompasses Baton Rouge headquarters. Major allegedly was a licensed gun dealer. According to the source, there was an auction of LDWF-seized guns on November 17, 1984. According to this source, Major allegedly bought three guns for 205 dollars while one gun alone was valued at one thousand dollars according to the source. The informant gave me serial numbers of the guns to substantiate his story. Once again, listen to all you hear. This major was indicted earlier on twelve counts of criminal violations by the Baton Rouge Federal Grand Jury. He was acquitted on all counts.

On September 4, 1987, two of my loyal agents quit, citing they could not take the pressure anymore.

Due to my letter-writing skills, on October 19, 1987, turncoat Major Flip and Flop asked for my assistance in writing a letter to Colonel Ram. I disguised the letter by giving it Major Flip and Flop's crude flair. Colonel Ram had no inkling that I had written the letter.

Major Flip and Flop thanked me for the letter stating he was going to "stick it" to the colonel.

On November 16, 1987, other agents, anonymously, gave information to Bob Marshall of the Times-Picayune newspaper in New Orleans. The article concentrated on the colonel and his practices. On November 19, 1987, Colonel Ram, very upset, called a meeting of Region 8, the entire portion of Southeast Louisiana of which District 8B consisted. Colonel Ram, embarrassingly, went piece-by-piece through the article. The colonel wanted to know who gave the information. All eyes turned on me; however, I stated if it would have been me I would have used my name and not taken the cowardly anonymous way. The mysterious group had accused the colonel of fixing tickets. The colonel shouted, "If I am fixing tickets, then charge me." The colonel lost his cool out of frustration. On December 11, 1987, the colonel called me and talked for one and a half hours. He dejectedly told me he could not take any more criticism and had decided to resign. He asked why I had written so many letters on him. He said, "You can't get anywhere like that." His tone of voice was total defeat.

Colonel Resigns amid Accusations

One might ask why the colonel would call me admitting defeat and telling of his plans to resign. One reason might be he would still need me because of a future business venture after retirement. According to a newsletter of the Louisiana Oyster Dealers and Growers Association and the Louisiana Oyster Task Force, Colonel Ram told the group he was retiring and setting up a company that would patrol their oyster leases for a fee. The ulterior motive for his talk with me was to try to smooth over our adversarial attitudes toward one another. Colonel Ram would need the cooperation of the local supervisors within LDWF enforcement in order to succeed in his newfound venture. Colonel Ram faded away without fanfare. Lieutenant Colonel Cook took over the role as colonel.

CHAPTER 18

New Governor with Old Ties

1988 began with a new governor, who envisioned new dreams with promises. However, his father had ties with Governor Rico, which made me a bit more apprehensive. Fresh off the chaos of the "epistle," the new appointees to the Department of Wildlife and Fisheries were certainly handicapped. Who would they listen to? Who would they believe? Would they genuinely try to fix the enquiries, or would it be a good-old-boy administration? I was very cautious about the new administration while waiting in the dark for a new ray of light. The media across the state had the "epistle" and began to press Secretary Icicle about her plans to change the corrupt practices of the past. Many in the press targeted certain high positions, which needed to be addressed or replaced.

There was an ongoing federal investigation of the sheriff of assumption parish and the use of bait during a dove hunt. Federal Agent Bill Melor and I met with the assistant United States attorney in New Orleans. The AUSA stated he would prosecute all federal violations discovered in the "epistle."

Empty Skies

On the front page of the Saint Paul Pioneer Express Newspaper was a large picture of me and two other agents posing with 168 ducks taken over bait illegally in Terrebonne Parish. The case was made on January 9, 1988. Dennis Anderson, the reporter, caught me off guard one early morning, and I unloaded on him about the abusive practices in Louisiana riddled with corrupt politics as it pertained to ducks. Ironically, I had not checked a legal hunter that year. I shrugged the interview off as being the typical reporter looking for a story. I was very wrong. The story not only circulated in Louisiana but also throughout several states in the Midwest. I began receiving letters of support from everywhere.

The criticism was aimed at the Ducks Unlimited Organization members who I had caught. In this article, a wealthy businessman, Ducks Unlimited National trustee, stated, "I did not stop at a limit from the first time I began hunting as a kid, until I was caught, nor did I know anyone else that did stop." This revelation was not news to me. This article smoked for quite some time, having lasting effects, as the future would reveal.

February 13, 1988

Col. [REDACTED]
Chief, Division of Enforcement
Louisiana Dept. of Wildlife and Fisheries
400 Royal St.
New Orleans, LA 70130

Dear Col. Montet:

Beginning on February 7, 1988 the St. Paul Pioneer Press Dispatch, St. Paul, MN ran a series of four articles entitled "Empty Skies: America's Ducks in Crisis." The series was authored by Dennis Anderson, Outdoor Editor, and deals primarily with illegal waterfowl hunting activities, particularly in Louisiana. Mr. Anderson apparently interviewed several Louisiana Law Enforcement personnel and Fish and Wildlife Service Special Agents in preparing to write his story. I am enclosing these articles for your review and comment.

By duplicity and innuendo, Mr. Anderson attempts to impinge the integrity and wetlands conservation milestones of Ducks Unlimited by portraying DU as an organization that looks the other way at waterfowl hunting violations. This is absolutely not true. We all make mistakes in life and hopefully learn from them, but when Mr. Anderson implies that DU is part of the enforcement problem, he belittles the herculean efforts by our 600,000 plus members in helping to halt the loss and further degradation of our continental wetlands.

This series of articles is already having an impact on Minnesota Ducks Unlimited. We are receiving numerous telephone calls and letters from our members and others appalled by what Anderson has said about waterfowl hunting violations in your state and the inability of your division and Fish and Wildlife Service Agents to significantly impact these activities.

As the contents of Anderson's articles become known and more widely distributed, I would anticipate that your agency will be the focus of similar inquiries that will necessitate public comment and/or news releases. I would appreciate receiving any official statements made by the Louisiana Dept. of Wildlife and Fisheries in regard to the enclosed articles.

133

No one defended DU more staunchly than Dale Whitesell, and Dale was not about to give free publicity to someone who took pot shots at the organization he so dearly loved. Stubborn and bull-headed, yes; nefarious and turncoat to the ducks, never.

I shared a number of points with Mr. Anderson -- none of which ever appeared in his article. I told him that other articles about ethics had been printed in our magazine since 1977, and that we have had long-standing plans to run an editorial on hunting ethics with a companion feature in our upcoming September/October issue. We selected this issue in the belief that its timing would have the most impact on behavior in the field. I told him of the Greenwing program which is designed to instill an appreciation for waterfowl and for the law in our youth. I know of no other program which is as exclusively devoted to training young hunters in ethical behavior as our Greenwing program. I told him of our waterfowl identification video guide which is unique in its approach to helping hunters hunt wisely and legally through sophisticated identification techniques.

I also told Mr. Anderson that Special Agent Dave Hall had some time ago been invited to address our winter staff meeting (February 25-28) so that all field staff will be better informed about the enforcement activities and challenges of the Fish and Wildlife Service.

In addition, I relayed to Mr. Anderson a conversation I had several weeks ago with Frank Dunkle, Director of the Fish and Wildlife Service. In this conversation, I congratulated Director Dunkle on his new emphasis on enforcement and expressed DU's belief that enforcement is a crucial priority for the Service. Director Dunkle is well aware of DU's concern about illegal harvests and our support for his efforts in this area.

Let's keep this matter in its proper perspective. Ducks Unlimited has been built on a sole purpose; that is, to secure and enhance habitat for waterfowl. We are not an enforcement agency. Enforcement of laws is a federal government responsibility which is shared with state governments at the discretion of the federal government. Ducks Unlimited and other private organizations are not empowered, nor should they be, to take enforcement matters into their own hands.

Ducks Unlimited, as a private organization, certainly can and does support and abide by these laws. You should not have any reason to doubt the commitment DU has to the laws of the land which have been designed to perpetuate two national heritages -- waterfowl and waterfowling.

Ducks Unlimited, too, has a proud heritage which it must perpetuate. Your support is that heritage. I pledge to you a commitment to uphold the responsibility your dedication deserves.

Please share this information with your DU co-workers. Thank you.

MBC:mep

NATIONAL HEADQUARTERS
One Waterfowl Way
Long Grove, IL 60047
(312) 438-4300

February 10, 1988

TO: DU Officers and Area Chairmen

FROM: Matthew B. Connolly, Jr. *Matt*

SUBJECT: ARTICLE - ST. PAUL PIONEER PRESS DISPATCH

This past Sunday, the St. Paul Pioneer Press Dispatch ran an article entitled "Empty Skies: America's Ducks in Crisis." As the first in a series authored by Outdoor Editor Dennis Anderson, the article deals with illegal take, particularly in Louisiana.

Ducks Unlimited is accused, unjustifiably, of "ignoring" a practice which all of us committed to waterfowl conservation abhor. A number of you who have seen the article have expressed concern to our field staff. Those of you who have not, may well hear about the piece and be asked about DU's policy on hunting ethics. Before this matter gets blown out of proportion, I would like to set the record straight.

Mr. Anderson's article refers to a former DU trustee charged with exceeding bag limits. This individual did not serve the duration of his trusteeship with DU because his colleagues did not see fit to renominate him. As an organization whose singular purpose is the conservation of waterfowl habitat, Ducks Unlimited has had a long-standing policy of demanding compliance, by its officers and employees, with regulations governing the harvest of waterfowl. This is a policy we uphold without equivocation.

The particular incident the author cites as evidence of DU's duplicity is an article involving a federal fish and wildlife agent which was written for Ducks Unlimited magazine in 1985. I personally authorized the undertaking of this magazine assignment. The article was a "human interest" feature on the day in a life of a federal fish and wildlife enforcement agent. It was not an exposition on the scope of illegal harvesting in Louisiana. Ducks Unlimited has never been presented with information detailing widespread abuses of hunting in any area of the country.

The article was never printed -- as is the case, I might add, with a number of articles which are prepared for the magazine. The decision not to print this article had nothing to do with DU's unwillingness to confront a controversial issue. Quite the contrary, our magazine has carried a number of articles on hunting ethics in the past decade. This year's September/October issue will feature another article which will strongly reiterate DU's stance on hunting ethics.

The reason the story in question was never published had to do with a different -- and equally admirable -- set of convictions. The agent featured in the story had been critical of DU's habitat work.

Most disturbing to me as past Minnesota Ducks Unlimited State Chairman, is the fact that while the waterfowl hunting violations cited in the articles are undoubtedly true and indicate that we must all work together to help alleviate the problem, I am equally concerned about federal and state law enforcement agents pointing fingers at DU members painting them all black with the same bottle of Dennis Anderson ink. This is a grave injustice and will more than likely impact DU's wetlands conservation programs in this state and elsewhere.

On a more personal note, I have hunted in your great state on several occasions. I recently spent a few mornings in the marsh with Carl Jones at the "Bismarck", and at the "4-Square Duck Club", DU members Bill Atkins, Pat Beaird, Jim Haynes and Lee Hawley showed this Minnesotan a thing or two about waterfowl hunting in Louisiana. In every case, whether we had 1, 2, 3 birds or a legal limit, we concluded our hunting activities by 10:00AM to noon, had the proper licenses and used plugged shotguns.

In some ways the articles seem unfair because they seem to imply that illegal waterfowl hunting is a "way of life" in Louisiana. My personal hunting experiences with the above gentlemen indicate that this is not so.

In closing, please find a copy of Mr. Matt Connolly's letter to DU officers and area chairmen in Minnesota. This letter provides the Ducks Unlimited response in regard to the Anderson articles.

Sincerely,

Warren R. Stefanski
Past State Chairman and
Chm., Minn. DU State Council

5 enclosures

cc. Mr. Len W. Samuelson, DU Nat'l./Internat'l. Relations
    Mr. Dan Baasen, DU Vice-Pres., N. Mississippi Flyway
    Mr. Gene Grazzini, Minnesota DU State Chairman
    Mr. Joe L. Herring, Chief, Division of Game, Louisiana Dept.
       of Wildlife and Fisheries

On Tuesday, March 15, 1988, I was called to Baton Rouge by supporters of the new governor. They were also members of the GCCA. These GCCA members had given the "epistle" to civil and criminal attorneys in order to dissect potential charges arising from the same. These people also discussed giving Secretary Icicle two weeks to take serious action within the ranks of the enforcement division. Their efforts centered on the colonel. Earlier, they met with the Lieutenant Colonel, who made self-serving statements such as "You get rid of Colonel Ram, and the problem with Chauvin goes away." Lieutenant Colonel Cook failed to mention that he wanted to be colonel.

I placed very little credence to the statement boasting about their ability to get to the governor directly. They said if Secretary Icicle did not act soon, they would begin another media blitz reintroducing the "epistle." They also mentioned suing the department if all else failed. One of these individuals from GCCA became chairman of the Louisiana Department of Wildlife and Fisheries commission. One drawback to his credibility was that he was originally appointed to the commission by Governor Rico.

On March 28, 1988, Secretary Icicle called me to set up a meeting at 8:30 a.m. on April 6, 1988. Secretary Icicle and Deputy Secretary Preppy would attend the meeting. The meeting was to be secret. Does that sound familiar? One must take into account that Secretary Icicle was originally appointed to the department as assistant secretary by Governor Rico. On April 6, 1988, we met. The meeting began with the bashing of department attorney Spirit of the Law, who gave politically convenient answers when he interpreted the law. I explained to Secretary Icicle and Deputy Secretary Preppy that I had attended numerous meetings of this nature, and they were designed to extract information rather than be used to remedy the situation. Deputy Secretary Preppy became defensive, due to his attorney background, and began taking notes. I told the Secretary and Deputy Secretary they were new to this, but I wasn't. I told them both they would have to prove their worth to me. I stated they knew how I stood by the files they had in their possession. Secretary Icicle stated that I had made some serious accusations in the past. I told her the accusations were facts supported by evidence. Icicle turned to Preppy asking, "Can he do that?" He told Icicle I had proven my cases well beyond speculation. I told Secretary Icicle and Deputy Secretary Preppy the files probably had been purged of such investigations as the diesel theft, agents violating shrimp laws, fixing tickets, unattended gill nets, threats, retaliation, kid's scheme by colonel, and continued interference by Senator BB.

Secretary's Friend under Grand Jury Investigation

Lastly, I told the Secretary and Deputy Secretary that her friend, Seafood Chief Ferret, was under investigation as we spoke. Icicle stated, "Not Porky." Deputy Secretary Preppy said it was his duty as well as hers to file charges with the district attorney. I did not elaborate on the Ferret case. Secretary Icicle was overwhelmed at my findings. She seemed to be confused and grasping overhead for answers.

On April 8, 1988, I met again with Deputy Secretary Preppy, who told me I should try to refrain from talking about the department in the media. My first impression was asking myself, "Was the facade cracking?" Deputy Secretary Preppy asked what were my orders from Secretary Snake-Eyes pertaining to the media. I explained that I requested orders in writing pertaining to the media, but Secretary Snake-Eyes declined to do so. I could see Deputy Secretary Preppy wanted me to stop talking to the media but was reluctant. Smart move on his part because my rule was to expose corruption.

Oyster Scam

One would expect that the members of the old regime would have learned their lesson about challenging my tenacity to be fair and honest in law enforcement. Be that as it may, another episode was peeking over the horizon. This case was another complicated example of selective enforcement that mushroomed with negative publicity about the Department of Wildlife and Fisheries. On September 10, 1987, commissioned agents from the LDWF issued a citation to A.C. for taking undersized oysters from state grounds. The legal size limit is three inches from hinge to mouth and fishermen are allowed 5 percent undersized oysters to be processed in the samples. The citation was the result of 24.9 percent undersized oysters. Twenty-three sacks of oysters were returned to the water as a result of the investigation. Later that day, in the same area, the agents boarded another vessel and discovered 23.7 percent undersized oysters. A citation was issued to the captain of the vessel, L.V. During the citation writing, agent Galloway was summoned to the vessel's radio room several times. The first call came from the owner of the vessel, who told Galloway he did not have enforcement authority. Calloway was then summoned to the radio by his immediate supervisor, R.H. R.H. stated Major Flip and Flop, in New Orleans enforcement, wanted another ten sacks sampled. RH's instructions went further by ordering Galloway to sample fifteen sacks. Galloway followed instructions and found 22.6 percent undersized oysters in the fifteen sacks sampled.

L.V., captain of the vessel, again summoned agent Galloway to the radio. Assistant Secretary Ferret of the Department of Wildlife and Fisheries instructed Galloway to dump just the small oysters and give L.V. a warning. His instructions were, "Don't give any more breaks and don't write a ticket to L.V."

On September 12, 1987, a citation was issued to P.B. for undersized oysters, 27.7 percent, in which seventeen sacks were seized and returned to the water.

On September 15, 1987, the owner of the vessel captained by L.V. called me to complain about the situation. The owner stated he called Major Flip and Flop and Galloway on September 10, 1987, to stop them from issuing a citation and not dumping oysters. The owner stated he then called Assistant Secretary Ferret, who allegedly assured the owner that things would be taken care of. The owner said, as a result of that call to Ferret, he was allowed to keep his oysters. In talking to the owner, it was alleged the owner of the vessel and Ferret were taking a trip to Florida the following week. The owner stated, "Maybe I should not have told you that. That sounds bad, doesn't it?" I knew the owner well, but he did not know me as well as he thought. He wanted my seal of approval and did not get it.

On September 16, 1987, in an unusual move, I received the controversial cases and citations via certified mail from R.H. I would usually pick up the charges in person from his office. The unwritten message connoted the severity of the whole situation in which R.H. did not want to be the pawn. In this package of charges and citations, I noticed that the citation written to L.V. was missing. On September 24, 1987, I questioned R.H. about the missing citation. R.H. stated he was following orders from Assistant Secretary Ferret, his boss. On September 29, 1987, I called R.H. demanding the L.V. citation. R.H. said he could not find the citation. Here we go. R.H. also stated that the owner of the vessel captained by P.B. wanted to know why his competitor was allowed to keep his oysters and his were dumped—a legitimate question. Allegedly, on October 7, 1987, there was a meeting in Baton Rouge in which Seafood Chief Ferret ordered the citations against P.B. not to be filed. The plot thickens. R.H. pointed out the inconsistency in dumping and not dumping oysters as well as his fear of being sued. R.H. told me Ferret stated, "Don't worry about a lawsuit." The new orders from Ferret allegedly were to give 20 percent undersized oysters in violation of the law. Ironically, the subjects in question were all over 20 percent undersized. Embarrassingly, Galloway stated he was ordered to go to the fishermen telling them no charges would be filed. According to Galloway, L.V. stated, "That's what you get for f——ing with my boss." Everyone knowing my attitude about this type of corruption, especially selective enforcement, tried to slip undetected out of the mess. R.H. kept placing in writing his current orders. Not only was he mitigating liability on his part but also giving me written documentation in my investigation. R.H. now sent me a memo with citations and offense reports attached stating higher authorities asked these three citations not be processed.

Dear Mr. ██████,

Over the past years I have tried to maintain a consistent enforcement effort to avoid confusion and selective enforcement practices. The only way one can maintain respect is to follow the letter of the law and when that is done by subordinates, he should expect the support of his supervisors. However, I find that most supervisors do not have the guts to say <u>NO</u> to politically affluent people .

For the past two years I have criticized these practices even to the point that I have had to file a formal Grievance through the Chain of Command which resulted in a Grievance Hearing that was chaired by Mr. ██████. The 90-minute hearing scoped the political influence and pressures placed on supervisors by outside parties, inter-departmental politics, illegal orders, and the harassment of those who try to do their jobs honestly and fairly across the board. Predictably, many questions were left unanswered throughout the Grievance process because the answers were requested in writing.

Even though I was threatened with my position I continued to ask questions which were morally and legally sound in order to do an effective job. I feel that I have the moral responsibility to treat everyone the same. Similarly, I have the legal duty to report ALL criminal violations to the District Attorney with proper jurisdiction. To tamper with this system violates the core of the criminal justice system. I do not blame the outside parties, but rather Department personnel who chose to prostitute their convictions for whatever reason.

Approximately five years ago I was questioned by a State Commission about alledged orders from the hierarchy not to enforce the law on ██████ employees in Lake Mechant. In addition, last year the hierarchy of the Oyster and Enforcement Divisions set up special patrols in the same area without results and without my knowledge allegedly to "catch Captain Chauvin in the act of not doing his job". I feel that this was part of the harassment for filing the Grievance. I have personally taken more oysters from ██████ than any other agent, however, these people respect my position and judgement in such matters, because they are people of good character and I am sure they will understand my position now.

In particular, with respect to your request per memo (attached) of October 12, 1987 to not process citations for undersized oysters, I cannot comply. First of all, I believe that the facts of all the cases submitted have definitely substantiated enough evidence to establish a violation of Title 56, Section 433 A. "...Any excess of over five percent of dead shells and oysters under the size prescribed herein (3 inches), in any cargo lot of oysters, shall be considered a violation of this subpart.

In conjunction with the aforementioned, the request from the hierarchy of the Oyster Division to give the fishermen up to 20% undersize oysters is in my opinion illegal. Ironically, the particular cases submitted were all above 20% undersize (see reports). Sister Lake personnel were adhering to instructions to give 20% and still found themselves not getting the backing for doing their jobs.

Major ███████████ informed me that he instructed Sister Lake personnel to take samples from 15 sacks of oysters and if found undersize then dump the whole cargo and cite the boat captain. You identified the higher authority as Mr. ███████████ who allegedly informed you to give ███████████ fisherman a break and issued instructions not to dump the oysters. However, similar discretion was not used on Mr. ███████████ and Mr. ███████████, 23 and 17 sacks, respectively of oysters undersize which were returned to the waters and citations issued. Mr. ███████████, ███████████ fisherman allegedly, was allowed to keep 315 sacks of oysters and only the sample was returned to the water and the citation not to be filed.

In retrospect, I feel that these practices discriminate against all those who have received citations for undersize oysters and have been convicted for less severe offenses of the same. Also, I have worked with Sister Lake personnel and I believe that all of their actions are in good faith and done for the betterment of the resource. To acquiesce in such matters can be misinterspreted as condoning such travesties, therefor, in order to protect the integrity of the Enforcement Division and the Sister Lake personnel I feel these cases should be processed. In the future, I would ask that everyone involved in such indiscretions, not place me in a position where I am asked to compromise my beliefs because I am very predictable when it comes to that...I will go by the LAW.

Requesting your cooperation in this and future matters, I remain...

Captain Roy Chauvin
Supervisor of District 8B
Enforcement Division

SECRETARY
(504) 820-5617

GOVERNOR

12 October 1987

M E M O R A N D U M

TO: Capt. Roy Chauvin, Enforcement Division

FROM: ~~————————~~ *RH₃₇₄₈*, CSA-V Study Leader

SUBJECT: Citations number 73727, 73729 and 73731

Higher authorities have asked that these three citations not be processed. All involve the harvest of undersized oysters during the opening days (10 and 12 September 1987) of the 1987-88 oyster season in Bay Junop. Particulars are as follows:

1. Citation number 73727 – ~~————————————~~.
Twenty-three sacks of undersized oysters (24.9%) were returned to the water.

2. Citation number 73729 – ~~————————————~~.
Undersized oysters from 15 sacks were returned to the water. Legal oysters from those sacks and all oysters from the remaining 315 sacks were allowed to enter the market. Oysters from the 15 counted sacks ran 22.5% undersize.

3. Citation number 73731 – ~~————————————~~. Seventeen sacks of undersized oysters (27.7%) were returned to the water.

Sorry for the trouble. If you need any additional information, give me a call.

CC: ~~————————~~
~~————————————~~
Enforcement File
File

State of Louisiana

DEPARTMENT OF WILDLIFE AND FISHERIES
ENFORCEMENT DIVISION
P.O. BOX 98000
BATON ROUGE, LOUISIANA 70898
504 925-4012

January 8, 1988

M E M O R A N D U M

TO: MAJOR ████████ SUPERVISOR REGION 8

FROM: COLONEL ████████
         CHIEF-LAW ENFORCEMENT

SUBJECT: MEMO REPLY/CAPTAIN ROY CHAUVIN-NOVEMBER 1
         NOT PROCESSING CITATIONS

I have reviewed Captain Chauvin's memo dated November 1 referencing
citations, #73727, 73729, 73731 and 73732. Please see that the charges
associated with these citations are filed with the District Attorney in
the court of jurisdiction.

Upon completion,please have Captain Chauvin advise me by letter that
the charges have been filed.

If you have any questions, please contact me.

RAM/crl

xc: ████████, Secretary
     ████████ Assistant Secretary
     ████████ Legal Counsel
     Major ████████
     Captain Roy Chauvin ✓

144

State of Louisiana

DEPARTMENT OF WILDLIFE AND FISHERIES
DISTRICT VIII
400 ROYAL ST.
NEW ORLEANS, LA 70130

The Honorable Doug Greenburg
Terrebonne Parish District Attorney
400 East Main
Courthouse Annex
Houma, LA 700360

Dear Mr. Greenburg:

Please disregard the work "Void" written across the enclosed Citations

#73731 and #73732. Captain Chauvin will explain the reason and why

these charges are so late.

Sincerely,

Major ███████
Supervisor, Region VIII
Enforcement Division

JM/ks   January 19, 1988

                                         Roy,

                                         Please call me as soon as you get

                                         this.

                                                        JOE

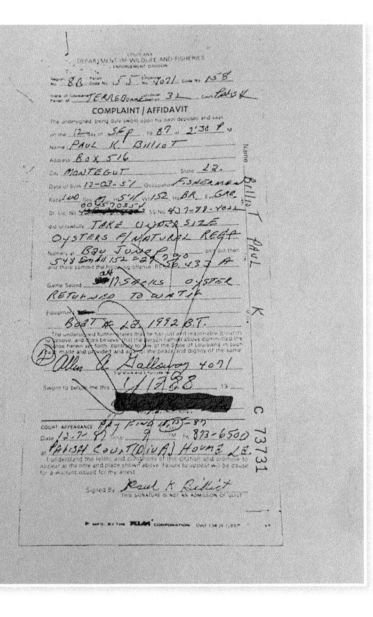

LOUISIANA
DEPARTMENT OF WILDLIFE AND FISHERIES
ENFORCEMENT DIVISION

86   55   7071   158

TERREBONNE   32

COMPLAINT / AFFIDAVIT

The undersigned, being duly sworn upon his oath deposes and says:

on the 12 day of SEP 19 87 at 2:30 P M

Name PAUL K. BILLIOT

Address BOX 516

City MONTEGUT   State LA.

Date of Birth 12-03-57   Occupation FISHERMAN

Race W.   Sex M   Ht 5'11   Wt 152   Hr BR   Eyes GRE.

Dr. Lic No. 0035-70357   SS No. 437-78-7071

did unlawfully TAKE UNDER SIZE
OYSTERS F/NATURAL REEF
Name of BAU JUDE P   and did then
548 Sm. All 152 = 24 270
and there commit the following offense RS. 56. 433 A

Game Seized 17.5 SACKS OYSTER at
RETURNED TO WATER

Equipment
BOAT # LA 1992 B.T.

The undersigned further states that he has just and reasonable grounds to believe, and does believe that the person named above committed the offense herein set forth, contrary to law of the State of Louisiana in such case made and provided and against the peace and dignity of the same.

Allen Q. Halloway 7071
Signature and Unit No.

Sworn to before me this 1/12/88 19

COURT APPEARANCE PAY FINE (X) 15-87

Date 12-7-87   Time 9   Ph. 873-6500

at PARISH COURT (DIV A) HOUMA LA.

I understand the terms and conditions of this citation and promise to appear at the time and place shown above. Failure to appear will be cause for a warrant issued for my arrest.

Signed By Paul K Billiot
THIS SIGNATURE IS NOT AN ADMISSION OF GUILT

MFD. BY THE KLM CORPORATION DWF 156 (R. 1-80)

C 733731

Name Billiot Paul K.

Exhibit 14

CERTIFIED MAIL
RETURNED RECEIPT REQUESTED

TO: COLONEL ████████

FROM: CAPTAIN ROY CHAUVIN

SUBJECT: REPLY AS ORDERED IN JANUARY 8, 1988 MEMO TO MAJOR
████████████

Dear Colonel ██████,

On January 21, 1988 I met with Mr. Greenburg as ordered by you
in your letter of January 8, 1988 (exhibit 1), to discuss
oyster violations that had not been filed by way of the normal
process. In addition, I tried to explain to Mr. Greenburg the
reason(s) for the word "VOID" written across two of the citations.
Mr. Greenburg was not pleased with the method in which these
citations were handled throughout the process, in that there
were inconsistent and selective enforcement practices. Mr.
Greenburg stated that he would prosecute the cases and any
other related cases.

Colonel ██████, I do not think that this entire matter was
handled properly from the beginning. Now, I feel as though
I am being used to exonerate those who have betrayed the criminal
justice system. As supervisor of District 8B I do not feel
as though you should have placed me in another precarious
situation such as this with respect to the questioning of
alleged illegal actions of department personnel, including,
but not limited to Assistant Secretary ████████████. You
should have intervened when I initially objected to this
problem in my letter to Major ██████████ on September 27, 1987
(exhibit 2). Instead you chose to remain silent even though
I was told by Major ████████ on October 5, 1987 that the charges
against ████████████████████ were not to be filed on orders from
████████████. Major ████████ said he did not agree with ██████,
but he would respect his orders as Assistant Secretary.
Then on October 12, 1987 I received a memo (exhibit 3) from
████████████ requesting that all 3 undersize oyster cases not
be processed, even though more than enough evidence was present
to establish a clear violation. This request was the result
of an October 7, 1987 meeting with ████████████, ████████████,
████████████, and Allen Galloway. According to sources this
meeting was held in Baton Rouge specifically to discuss these
particular oyster cases in question. It was at this time that
Major ████████ informed me that you did not want the charges
filed. Major ████████ also informed me that he had received a
written request from ████████████ that the charges not be filed
against anyone of the three violators. Major ████████ informed
me that the citations were voided at this time.

On November 1, 1937 I wrote a letter to ▓▓▓▓▓▓▓ questioning illegal orders and not filing citations (exhibit 4). On December 9, 1987 Major ▓▓▓▓▓▓ informed me that you were very upset over the letter and that the charges would not be filed. Then on Friday, December 11, 1987 you called at the Region 8 office criticizing my method of handling said case. You stated that ▓▓▓▓▓▓▓ was wrong, but I should have stayed out of the decision and let ▓▓▓▓▓▓▓▓ file the charges. You told me that you were not going to file the charges and you speculated that Allen Galloway and ▓▓▓▓▓▓▓▓▓▓ would change their statements and would not testify. You stated, "...you are pissing off a lot of important people again---people who can help you". You reminded me that "this is the way the system works and letters like this can't change the system". You stated that ▓▓▓▓▓▓▓ made a mistake, but "▓▓▓▓ has no choice but not to file the charges because he did not take the oysters".

Again on December 14, 1987 Major ▓▓▓▓▓▓ stated he was told not to file the charges by you.

It is my understanding that on December 14, 1987 in the New Orleans office there was a meeting between Mr. ▓▓▓▓▓, ▓▓▓▓▓, ▓▓▓▓▓, Major ▓▓▓▓▓, and you to discuss the case. It is my understanding that ▓▓▓▓▓▓▓▓ said the case against ▓▓▓▓▓▓▓▓ fisherman was a bad one and stood by his decision not to file the charges. It is also my understanding that Major ▓▓▓▓▓▓ asked who was going to take responsibility for the charges not being filed because he felt the charges were valid. Major ▓▓▓▓▓ request for written orders, in my understanding were denied. Major ▓▓▓▓▓ was left out on a limb much like Allen Galloway and ▓▓▓▓▓▓▓▓▓▓.

Colonel ▓▓▓▓▓, this case was made on September 10, 1937 and the charges were not filed until January 21, 1988. Don't you think that it would have been much easier to go by the law in the first place and not give special consideration to so called "important people"? Don't you think it would have been legally sound to book Allen Galloway, ▓▓▓▓▓▓▓▓, Major ▓▓▓▓▓, and me initially, so as not to create an atmosphere of intimidation and uneasiness at the bottom rung of the ladder? Don't you think that enforcing the law indiscriminately is the honest and ethical thing to do? I find it very difficult to understand why this Department would continually go through the unnerving rigors of a cover-up rather than condescend to the simple system of justice for all. I firmly believe that had I not objected to these illegal orders that the charge would never have been filed on ▓▓▓▓▓▓▓▓, who is a second offender for undersize oysters (exhibit 5). Also I believe that similar charges would have been filed on ▓▓▓▓▓▓▓ and ▓▓▓▓▓▓▓ during this selective enforcement process. Colonel ▓▓▓▓▓, to say that this is the way the system works and it cannot be changed is a rationalized escape from your duty to ensure equal protection under the law. WE ARE THE SYSTEM, IF IT IS WRONG, WE ARE WRONG.

Colonel ████, this case was no different than the initial
278 page document filed with the Department on July 25, 1986
by certified mail and again on August 14, 1986 by Federal
Express after I did not receive a return receipt of the same.
In this document I enumerated outside influence and possible
criminal wrong-doing. This case is no different than the
████████, ███████, Jr., ██████████ and many other
cases that I cited in the document. These charges were never
filed by the Department through the normal channels, but all
were convicted trial or pled guilty. This case is no different
than the illegal orders concerning the inside-outside shrimp
line at Caminada Pass or any different than the illegal orders
pertaining to █████ and ██████████████ cases on unattended
gill nets and related charges, in which ██████████ pled guilty
to violations of Title 56 while ████████ and others were
found guilty of Title 56 violations at their trial. In this
case I was ordered by you to "give them a break if they were
half-ass trying". This case is no different than the illegal
orders not to enforce the size limit on crabs. This case is
no different than your orders not to seize shrimp boats in
violation of the law and the list goes on and on.

Colonel ████, also in our conversation of December 11, 1987
you questioned the timing of my report, implying that it was
politically motivated. I take exception to your statement in
that I have questioned these unfair practices for quite some
time. For example, In July of 1986 I filed a Grievance with
the Department to question the validity of some accusations
in my Civil Service rating of the previous year. In Step 2
of my Grievance you did not afford me an opportunity to voice
my viewpoint, in violation of the Grievance Process, and you
agreed with my evaluation, in particular Point 3 which dealt
with influence from outside parties. Said influence was
alleged not to be in conformity with the suggestions and
guidelines of the Department. At the Grievance hearing on
October 9, 1986, chaired by Mr. ██████████ I discovered that
he too agreed with Point 3. The outside parties were enumerated
as Judge Fanguy and District Attorney Douglas Greenburg, who
only suggested that I go by the law. On October 30, 1986 the
written results of the hearing were received by me and Mr. ████
concurred that I had been influenced by the same outside parties.
(exhibit 6).

Colonel ████, don't you feel as though we operate under a dual
standard which in actuality discriminated against me? The
facts show that ██████████████ would never have made this decision
had there not been influence from outside parties. This
influence was not to ensure that the law would be upheld, but
it was to ensure that criminal charges were not filed on
██████████████ and most important approximately $7,000 worth
of oysters were kept in violation of the law.

149

Colonel ████, I don't know if one could call these actions "ticket-fixing", but one could most definitely not call these actions fair and honest. My efforts are continually being obstructed to prohibit me from enforcing even the basic spirit and intent of the law. Recently, I have uncovered more evidence to show that document(s) were altered to conceal possible criminal wrong-doing, but as usual my complaints will most likely fall on deaf ears.

Once again, Colonel ████, I ask that you do not involve me in such indiscretions, which I feel are not honest or legal. I do respect important people' influence, but I am not willing to compromise my beliefs or succumb to the corrupt influencing as exhibited in the enumerated cases. I am not looking to create my own private oyster surveillance company. I am not looking for an Assistant Secretary's position. Nor am I seeking to be Chief of the Oyster Division. All I would ask is that the Department let me do my job honestly and fairly across the board, so that I can look at the public and not have to be embarrassed to be a wildlife agent.

Hoping you will help me to take the necessary steps for a better Enforcement Division in the near future, I remain....

Captain Roy Chauvin
Supervisor of Enforcement
Terrebonne and Lafourche Parishes

150

Overwhelming Problems and Under the Table Orders

On December 9, 1987, Major Flip and Flop told me Colonel Ram wanted me not to file the charges. After a great deal of pressure from the fishermen and the press, grand jury subpoenas were issued to AG and DC on April 22, 1988. On April 25, 1988, I spent four hours testifying before the secret grand jury hearings in Terrebonne Parish. As usual, the rats were trying to find out how bad the storm would be. Questions like, "Am I the target?" or "What was said about me?" were common. On May 20, 1988, the media wanted a statement from me and only me. Secretary Icicle said okay. Deputy Secretary Preppy tried to limit what I would say, and Colonel Ram said, "Go by the guidelines." Guidelines didn't exist. In June of 1988, Ferret was indicted by the State grand jury for numerous felony counts. The media continued to push the department accusing the current administration of not acting fast enough to remedy the problems. As a result of continued harassment, Colonel Ram announced his resignation.

The New/Old Dominion

The one who replaced Colonel Ram was Lieutenant Colonel Cook, who was very sneaky and had no loyalty to anyone but himself. An example of this self-centered characteristic was exhibited on the night before the "epistle" was published in the newspaper. Lieutenant Colonel Cook called me about twelve midnight asking if he was in the newspaper. He said, "I never did anything to you, did I?" It was as if he didn't know, or remember if he had any adverse dealings with me. This was a testament to his character that he wasn't loyal to anyone. He was a master at playing all sides during the changes of administrations. However, his first choice was the old Governor Rico administrations. During the Governor Romer Administration, he was out of his league. He was a yes-man intimidated by me and just waiting for the arrival of the next administration.

I never did trust Lieutenant Colonel Cook due to the fact that he always came out unscathed in most controversial situations, often shifting blame on incompetent subordinates. His tactic was to only promote and associate with those he could control. We never developed any kind of relationship. He would shield himself by placing a supervisor between him and me. Selling your soul to the devil was the order of the day. Eventually, you would be asked to do something that would make you feel uncomfortable due to the demands of legality, or immorality. I was a free spirit who never felt uncomfortable in my decisions as long as my conscience was my guide.

As the secrecy of the Ferret grand jury began to unravel, the questions asked were deeper than I first thought. Major Flip and Flop said that Baton Rouge headquarters told him to lie to the grand jury. The major asked for my advice about lying. It should have been self-explanatory, but aligning himself with me made him feel protected due to my relationship with the district attorney.

Major Flip and Flop said the department lawyers told him not to speak to me; however, he was told by someone to lie about me. It was a shame because this guy was basically a good person who was afraid to lose his job. He was very weak and easily manipulated. When he needed me, he was my friend, but when I was out on a limb with an outstretched hand for support, he was right there with them warming up his chainsaw.

The influence of the Rico Administration seemed to impede the efforts of the Roemer Administration, which was overwhelmed at the persistence of corporate individuals. On July 21, 1988, a very popular friend of the biologists was caught with a 2,400-foot-long gill net clearly in violation of the law. My immediate supervisor said not to cite the individual due to his friendship with the biologist. On the other hand, Deputy Secretary Preppy instructed me to cite the individual.

In an unprecedented move on July 27, 1988, I was called to Baton Rouge headquarters to attend an "administrative hearing" chaired by the violator's friend, Biologist Nero. This so-called hearing was an obvious attempt to circumvent the law. Biologists Nero had never dealt with me other than to have a cup of coffee together. We never squared off in a formal arena. Biologists Nero tried to interpret a law that he knew nothing about. His hearing was immediately derailed by me citing the letter of the law. I told those attending the hearing if a law was inadequate, then change it legislatively. Don't put pressure on me because I won't bend. Due to the inadequacy of those spearheading this "hearing," this tactic was never used again.

On August 8, 1988, there was a claim by fishermen that, once again, there was selective enforcement in Grand Isle, Louisiana, pertaining to the shrimp line. To refresh memories, I was replaced as supervisor of Grand Isle by the Rico Administration because I enforced the law. An ambitious subordinate of mine took over Grand Isle with disastrous effects. The people were demanding my reinstatement. I didn't need the headache but was subsequently placed in charge of Grand Isle again, raising eyebrows of the local fishermen.

On August 10, 1988, Terrebonne District Attorney informed the department he wanted clarification of a fish law. As a result, Deputy Secretary Preppy and Attorney Spirit of the Law differed the problem to Assistant Attorney General K.D. This was a move by Attorney Spirit of the Law to shirk his responsibilities. Attorney Spirit of the Law told me that I was always trying to jam the department with enforcing the law. Attorney Spirit of the Law stated that I would coax the district attorney to write these letters asking for clarification of the law. Attorney Spirit of the Law stated he was putting me on notice. I honestly did not know what he meant, nor did I care. He was a minnow going after a largemouth black bass. Under the table, Deputy Secretary Preppy told me to keep putting pressure on Attorney Spirit of the Law. Once again, sneaky tactics. Deputy Secretary Preppy was second-in-command within the department, yet he wanted me to do his job.

On October 31, 1988, and again on November 2, 1988, I attended a strategy meeting discussing how to get agents to go to work. I told them to stop protecting corrupt agents and enlist consequences. I brought up the diesel theft investigation involving Agent G. I posed the question, "How can you get respect when nothing is done?" The public saw this and said this administration was no better than the past. On November 21, 1988, Secretary Icicle blasted enforcement in the media saying only a few dedicated agents were working. Guilty agents were infuriated while the agents who worked were happy with her comments. Who do you think was in the majority?

1989

The infinite wisdom of the administration thought the enforcement division needed reorganization. My position was lieutenant with the same duties and responsibilities. This move changed nothing but created a couple of promotions. I was excluded from any promotions, not to my surprise.

Then an issue came up that I always wanted to address but did not have anything to do with enforcement personnel. For years, some biologists/helpers would take samples of hundreds of pounds of seafood for personal gain. On February 6, 1989, it was my understanding that a biologist/helper outside my area was caught with hundreds of pounds of black bass and lake runners during a sampling. To acquiesce during these abuses would never solve the problem. The administration, again, was overwhelmed, running around like chickens with their heads cut off.

One of the main obstacles in solving this problem was indicted Ferret, who continued to have a position of authority over the biologists. Although Ferret lost his authority over enforcement, the Rico Administration slipped him into another position, with authority no less. Ferret and Secretary Icicle were longtime friends. What else can I say. Secretary Icicle was also assistant secretary under the Rico Administration. Everyone buried their heads in the sand, not wanting to tackle that ever-present abuse. Excuse was that these practices have been going on forever, so what is wrong now? This brings me to an old Beatles song, "Let it be, let it be, these are words of wisdom, let it be."

In retaliation for bringing up the fish abuse case, biologists revealed that Deputy Secretary Preppy allegedly had just received fish from a routine operation to have a fry. The cloudy lines indicated that this fry may have been for the department, not personal, benefit. The question remains, ethical or unethical?

On February 23, 1989, the district attorney called me into his office on a complaint of selective enforcement of shrimp size laws. One dealer accused another dealer of being corrupt due to his ties with Ferret. This accused dealer, according to District Attorney, called him to help Ferret with his indictment. The DA frustratingly stated the number one complaint in his office was wildlife-related, not rape, murder, or drugs. The district attorney did not believe me, before he was elected, that he would be deluged with wildlife complaints.

Then again, on May 19, 1989, a sixty-one-foot-long shrimp vessel was seized in a shrimping violation in Senator BB's taboo area. My agents assisted Senator BB's agents, Bass and G, in dealing with the case. Senator BB's agents decided to sell the shrimp to Rox's Seafood. Sound familiar? A problem arose in the fact that the captain of the vessel culled some of the shrimp for sale. The captain later refused to cooperate by not culling the shrimp. Procedure for selling culled shrimp was followed; however, the problem arose when the senator's agents allegedly decided to give the remainder of the shrimp to the dealer. The shrimp should have been sold to the dealer at a lower price but were not, in violation of law and procedure. The department once again ignored the daunting facts: see no evil, hear no evil, speak no evil, must not be evil.

On May 22, 1989, there was a court hearing to release the sixty-one-foot-long vessel. The district attorney argued in court that the bond was illegal. I was ordered not to release the boat. On June 19, 1989, Captain Flip and Flop told me Colonel Cook had flipped sides on boat seizures, ordering me to release the boat. Deputy Secretary Preppy was unhappy with the colonel, but nothing was done. Attitudes within the department were beginning to change due to the fact that Governor Rico was going to run again, and the likelihood of him winning was high. The department's loyalties were being tested; however, everyone knew whose side they would take. Colonel Cook turned out to be a backstabbing coward.

Biologist's Corruption Overlooked

As if fate would have it, the biologist's problem was exposed in my area. According to sources, a finfish biologist named Booray was caught trolling for shrimp out of the state gill net boat for personal gain. Booray was not a shrimp biologist/helper. Booray had an eighty-four-quart- and forty-eight-quart ice chest full of shrimp, allegedly for "the freezer." Whose freezer was never revealed. On June 28, 1989, Captain Flip and Flop and Colonel Cook, like sharks smelling blood in the water, decided to attack the biologists. The hypocrites wanted me to bring the results of my investigation to headquarters on June 29, 1989. Deputy Secretary Preppy said he was thoroughly disgusted one episode after the other. One supervisor of the biologist said lots of biologists were going to be in trouble due to the widespread abuses. This issue died, so I thought. On November 21, 1989, I was chastised by Booray's supervisor in Bourg, Louisiana. The supervisor said his man was set up. Really? What a joke. On December 1, 1989, another high-ranking biologist in Baton Rouge had the department summon me in order to admonish me for causing problems with the biologists. This was the same supervisor that privately told me many biologists would be in trouble for this abuse. I could see the midterm administration was crumbling in chaos. The Rico tail began to wag the failing dog. Rico announced he will run again, and the department immediately began to embellish the future prospects of Déjà vu.

Agent of the Year

On August 19, 1989, a strange twist of events happened, which did not fool me for a second. I was bombarded by numerous accolades after being nominated by my department. I felt the enforcement division was nudged by the administration. I received the highest award an enforcement agent could receive, statewide agent of the year. I also received the Southeastern Association of Game and Fish Commission highest award, outstanding officer in the southeast. In addition, I received the prestigious Shikar Safari International Award for meritorious service in the field of wildlife conservation and law enforcement. Earlier, I received the outstanding service award from the Gulf Coast Conservation Association for dedicated service in law enforcement. Then I received the Terrebonne Sportsmen's league award for outstanding law enforcement.

I appreciated the awards outside the department's enforcement division. I thought the department had motives behind their selection of me. One reason was the outside pressure of powerful people in organizations who supported my efforts. Somehow, the department felt this would diffuse my efforts to continue my push to rid politics and corruption out of my job. The enforcement division granted the award in an effort to thwart my persistent letter writing and my contacts with the media. In my own way of protesting, I did not attend the convention in Saint Louis, Missouri, to receive the awards. Deep down, I felt the department was trying to buy my loyalty that was not for sale.

CHAPTER 19

Mix Bag

National Geographic Story

As a result of the press and awards, the National Geographic Society decided to do a TV story on my efforts. Susan Winslow of the TV division of the National Geographic Society headed the team of several people who followed me for one week. The whole crew trudged their way on a long cold boat ride walking in the swamp to film an actual duck case with thirty-three ducks taken over bait.

On January 7, 1990, we set up a massive operation employing the use of a roadblock in a strategic area to check for violations. This was an unprecedented method, which caught the public by surprise. I was in charge of the operation, which consisted of thirty federal and state agents all with specific duties. The primary targets were hunters returning from a weekend of hunting. A total of forty major cases were developed that day during the three-hour process.

During this one week, Susan Winslow and her crew rode in my car all day asking questions about our area. On the afternoon of the last day of filming, we drove to lower Lafourche Parish where Susan Winslow wanted my overall views of my career. As we stood in a very picturesque area, Susan Winslow asked a common question. Susan Winslow stated, "We know of your conviction and drive to take care of the little animals, but how sincere are you? How far would you go?" I told her, pointing to a levee where duck hunters leave their hunting ponds, "If President

Ronald Reagan came over that levee and had too many ducks, I would not hesitate to book him." That statement enlisted a smile from the entire crew. The one-hour documentary aired one year later with tremendous responses according to Susan Winslow. This was a very pleasant break from my intense life. My answers flowed freely seemingly with no pressure. I received absolutely no guidelines from the department on how to answer controversial questions. I guess the department feared I would tell the national media I was restricted on what I could say, then I would turn around and say what I felt was right anyway. My immediate supervisors quipped that I appeared to be the administration's "boy," adding all that can change with the next administration.

National Geographic Society

WASHINGTON, D.C. 20036

TELEVISION DIVISION

January 16, 1990

Mr. Roy Chauvin
Rt. 11, Box 5041
Gibson, Louisiana 70356

Dear Roy,

Many thanks for all your help with our film. Due in large part to you, our week in Louisiana turned out to be a real success. Even the weather cooperated against impossible odds (you didn't have anything to do with that, did you?).

You were so great to work with, Roy -- such a wealth of information and so accommodating about all of our various pain-in-the-neck requests. To cite only one example: driving all the way to Golden Meadow was way above and beyond the call of duty. It allowed us to keep to our schedule. I am most grateful for that favor and the many, many others along the way.

The film's not back from the lab yet but they've sent word that it's looking good. Fran shot a lot of stills as well, also not back. We're planning to send you a few when we get them. Also, of course, a tape of the finished film, but not for a year or so when it's all finally done. I'm sure I'll be talking to you before then for information to put into the script.

What you have done and are doing down there in Louisiana for wildlife is really remarkable. I only hope our film does justice to your work and that we too can help even a little in changing attitudes about the use and abuse of the "little animals." There aren't many people out there actually making a difference. You are one.

Best Wishes,

Susan Winslow

Lost Investigation

All of the accolades and attention disappeared on January 26, 1990, when I was assigned to work with J. W. of internal affairs to resurrect the investigation of the abuses of biologists as it pertained to sampling and disposition of samples.

The first interview was with a supervisor of the biologist, who stated earlier that a lot of biologists would lose their jobs if we investigated that issue. Now, on the record, the same supervisor did not remember saying anything in a prior meeting with us.

It has always been strange to me how people's memories seem to evade them during a crisis. An example of this would be Secretary Snake-Eyes who said that due to his stroke and lack of oxygen to the brain, he could not remember anything during his under oath testimony. Not under oath, though, he could chastise you quoting every word you said.

When someone tells you the truth during an investigation, you tend to be a little merciful; however, when they flat out lie, your blood boils, and your drive to expose them is overwhelming. So what would you prefer: a docile investigation with sympathy, or a tenacious investigator tearing apart everything coming out of your mouth? A good investigator usually knows the answer to most questions he asked, or will give the appearance of such.

Our investigation led J. W. and I to a seafood dealer in lower Lafourche Parish, who stated he was approached by the target of the investigation, biologist/helper Booray. The dealer said Booraay was trying to cover up any problems. We also interviewed another seafood dealer from lower Lafourche Parish who supplied us with receipts listing dates and times that Booray had sold shrimp to him. After the investigation was submitted, I heard nothing but resentment from biologists. Nothing happened to the target of the investigation even though there was overwhelming evidence. The practice probably still exists today. To the victor goes the spoils, shrimp and fish abound. The balance of the scales of justice seemed to be swinging back and forth rather than even keel. This was not new to me but was always a bitter pill to swallow. Decisions like these made me tougher and tougher and calloused my mindset.

It was public knowledge that the biologists were often told to bring seafood to Baton Rouge, especially during the Rico Administration. The biologist said many trips were made on state time. At times when samples weren't available, the biologists said they were ordered to go out and catch fish just to please the politicians. These runs had no scientific value at all, except to exacerbate the rotten policies and further frustrate the good employees who were few and far between.

Also, some enforcement agents from North Louisiana would say that they received orders from headquarters to go out and net crappie for department administrators. This act was highly illegal due to the fact that crappie were game fish. These acts were so brazen that these agents would come to South Louisiana to work shrimp patrols and bring a pickup truck with ice chests. Most of these agents did not want to work with me due to the fact that I did not allow them to take these shrimp home, or to headquarters, or to politicians.

One day, I observed a state representative back up to an agent's house and fill his Continental with several ice chests of shrimp that were seized from an illegal shrimping operation the night before.

On this night, an agent and I were on a large operation to seize nets being illegally used to shrimp during closed season. My efforts were done in response to the lady with the one can of pork and beans and her inspirational request. Approximately ten agents and five boats participated in the operation. The other agents sent by headquarters had intentions of filling up their ice chests with shrimp.

While I did things by the book on that night, we found a net being used illegally. The net was full of shrimp. As we began to release the shrimp, gunshots rang out in our direction causing us to seek cover behind a barge. Numerous shots were fired in the dark in our direction. The violators hid while waiting for us to show up. I immediately called for assistance on the radio. No one answered me. I called and called as shots rang out. No answer. To get out of our situation, I had to pass by a shrimp dock. It was 2 a.m. as we passed the infamous dock where the shots had originated. There were at least eight fishermen lined up along this dock all carrying guns. As I slowly moved past the dock in my boat, not a word was said. I instructed the young agent with me to unload all our guns in their direction if a shot was fired from the dastardly crew. We got by the dock without incident and headed to the boat landing to meet the other agents. As I approached the dock, I could see the agents loading up their ice chests with shrimp. One boat had approximately two thousand pounds of shrimp taken in closed season. As they separated their shrimp, I asked where was their radio. They began to search as I voiced my displeasure and found the radio beneath the two thousand pounds of shrimp. I told the agents what happened. They laughed and continued about their business of separating shrimp. I didn't complain to headquarters due to the fact that I overheard the agents saying how much shrimp headquarters would get.

As a result, the young agent working with me quit citing politics, rotten agents, and corruption throughout the department. The agent said that I was going to get killed one day due to these practices.

There was super frustration on my part due to the circumstances, but ringing out in my head was the lady with the five children and one can of pork and beans. I didn't work for the corrupt, I was not for sale, and I didn't give a quarter to the politicians. I worked for this poor lady who had no idea what I had to endure just to do my job.

District Attorney Loses Cool and Vents

On February 15, 1990, District Attorney D.G. unloaded on me about a myriad of problems, including, but not limited to, wildlife. The district attorney said he had just received a complaint from a reliable source on one of Senator BB's agents, Bass. Allegedly, Agent Bass brought 140 ducks illegally to the dock for his father-in-law. The district attorney also said he had lost a major case involving an influential person who allegedly gave a Cadillac to a judge for a favorable decision. I was personally a victim of the same judge rendering a favorable decision in a wildlife case. The defense lawyer told me he had given a diesel generator to the judge to be used at his camp. The lawyer said, while smiling, "This is the way the game is played. You can't compete with me." Then another influential person approached the district attorney for his help over one of my duck cases.

The district attorney asked me, in disgust, "How do you survive and maintain your reputation?"

I replied, "One must maintain consistency and honesty, never deviating regardless of criticism, or the dangling carrot."

Back in Grand Isle

On February 19, 1990, I attended a commercial fishermen's meeting in Galliano, Louisiana. I needed to start over by explaining my philosophy of law enforcement due to the fishermen's successful drive to replace me in Grand Isle during the Governor Rico Administration. The fishermen complained they were the subject of selective enforcement without me. Due to my reassignment to Grand Isle, I decided to meet with the Grand Isle fishermen as well to refresh their memories of my enforcement procedures. The Grand Island fishermen did not like the new shrimp line and wanted the old line back. Senator BB had changed the shrimp line to where the fishermen wanted to fish due to my strict enforcement. Now, the Grand Isle fishermen were upset because the new law had created too much competition. The good fishermen now were allowed to fish where the outlaws had a monopoly under the old law. Much to the dismay of the Grand Isle fishermen, I said I would enforce the new law. I told the fishermen from Grand Isle to watch out for what they asked for they might get it. I couldn't resist smiling at the fishermen.

Crabs and Crab Task

On March 1, 1990, I attended a crab task force meeting. Their major complaint was undersized crabs. Not long before, this same group criticized our crab size enforcement effort. It was determined by fishermen, the undersized crabs were flooding the market, decreasing profit. The biologist of the LDWF stated size enforcement would not help, or hurt the crab population. It was the biologists' opinion that you could not over fish crabs. Today, due to this philosophy, crabs in South Louisiana can cost up to five dollars per crab in any restaurant. In the old days, one would pay less than a dollar per dozen when crabs were plentiful. Well, I guess the biologists are eating crow today, certainly not crabs. On March 8, 1990, the judges of Lafourche Parish called for a meeting with me to get clarification of enforcement practices as they pertain to crabs. The judges seemed apprehensive, carefully selecting their words. I felt the meeting was held to determine any adverse effects that may arise in the media. Shortly thereafter, thousands of pounds of undersized crabs were seized. In a single incident, forty thousand pounds were seized from a dealer's eighteen-wheeler heading out of state.

Although somewhat of a dead issue, from time to time, the gill net crisis would resurface. On March 24, 1990, my agents seized five thousand feet of illegal nets. On May 17, 1990, there was a flip-flop in policies by the department, which infuriated the district attorney of Terrebonne Parish. Colonel Cook, Lieutenant Colonel Silver Tongue, and Deputy Secretary Preppy decided not to seize boats. This decision was concocted just prior to the opening of shrimp season. To say this move wasn't politically motivated was an understatement. Governor Rico was leading in the polls, and the administration needed to change tactics to compete. On May 18, 1990, agents issued fifty-one citations in conjunction with an undersized crab raid on a Lafourche Parish crab dealer. Then the crab task force changed its mind about undersized crab enforcement. The chairman of the crab task force made serious threats aimed at me, personally saying, "We are going to get you."

Roofing Nails

Coincidentally, on May 19, 1990, I found approximately fifty pounds of squarehead roofing nails scattered throughout my driveway. This act was personal; my home was off-limits to the corruption. This path of violence targeted my family's safety, which was totally unacceptable. Many people perceived me as a fearless fighter that no one could intimidate, but these cowardly acts were indefensible. I couldn't be everywhere all the time. In an attempt to stop this type of invasion of my private life, I initiated what I called the wrath of Roy era. I was very frustrated and I needed to bolster my image even stronger.

Phone Call Threat

Not long after this incident, I came home to my wife and daughter crying. My wife said, "Play your phone messages. There was a very chilling voice stating your husband will be dead within seven days." To make such statements in the heat of an investigation, face-to-face, is one thing. This was taken to a different level.

I conducted my own investigation into this matter, not trusting my deceiving department. I interviewed dealers and fishermen stating I would not accept this behavior, telling them I was tired of it. Most fishermen, although they did not like me, said that to involve my family was wrong. My intense investigation was closing in on a suspect and something totally unexpected happened. The suspect committed suicide, enhancing my fears that he was unstable enough to follow through with his threat. I kept this recording as a reminder that I was not invincible.

On June 6, 1990, things really heated up in Lafourche Parish. I was called in by the Lafourche Parish district attorney requesting a meeting over undersized crab enforcement. My attitude was still enshrouded by the wrath of Roy mission, making me less tolerable to criticism. The district attorney had been called out at the Lafourche Parish Rotary Club luncheon for lack of prosecution in several cases. The Rotary Club, mostly friends of mine, cited a series of thirty-three citations of which only one was prosecuted. The district attorney quickly blamed me for the statistics. The district attorney was also exposed, put on the carpet, for lack of prosecution on forty polluted oyster cases cited by the media. The district attorney, due to the different sources of criticism, reinstated the forty polluted oyster cases receiving convictions on all. The Lafourche Parish district attorney told me he would not allow me to run over him, like I did to the acquitted district attorney in Terrebonne Parish. The district attorney's vain attempt to criticize me only showed weakness on his part. He gave away his position. Now I could manipulate things around his vindictive attitude. One of the assistant district attorneys stated, "You are not our favorite person. You had better cool it." Well, I had been there and done that. My grandfather had a saying, "While they are talking, you aim."

On June 7, 1990, I met with District Attorney D.G. of Terrebonne Parish. He stated he was totally disgusted with the department, in particular, as they pertain to boat seizures. He stated he was experiencing a total lack of cooperation.

From September 24 through September 27, 1990, I attended a level-two supervisory school in Baton Rouge, Louisiana. I learned four things at this school enumerating the typical life of a law enforcement officer.

Statistically, the following exemplifies the life of a typical law enforcement officer:

1) married multiple times
2) abused wife and children

3) drinks to excess
4) die at fifty-five

What a life.

1991

The first half of 1991 seemed to be somewhat docile. I was able to do more fieldwork than I had done in the past. The administration had a hands-off policy. Only local skirmishes surfaced without any significant pressures. The new Lieutenant Colonel Silver Tongue seemed to want to befriend me. He wanted to gain the respect of my strong supporters in the public and especially the media. My supporters did not trust him, and I had to okay everything he said. This upset Silver Tongue. On January 17, 1991, Lieutenant Colonel Silver Tongue accompanied me to a GCCA meeting in Thibodaux, Louisiana. Silver Tongue tried to take over the meeting, but the crowd abruptly cut him off, asking for my answers to critical questions. This did not sit well with Silver Tongue, who continued to try to recruit me. Silver Tongue took my side on insignificant battles with agents but that effort was small time. I did not hear much from Silver Tongue when it came to larger battles with politicians.

On April 4, 1991, agents picked up thousands of feet of unattended gill nets in Senator BB's area, but there was no response from Senator BB. This was very strange; however, the reason was about to be made known.

This time, the department's general attitude was laid-back. Do nothing and nothing will happen. Grumblings of the old Rico Administration coming back next year was a source of gossip. Meanwhile, the current administration did not want to tackle any controversial issues. That would put egg on their faces. Thus, the quiet before the storm was inevitable.

CHAPTER 20

Alligators

Up to my Eyes in Alligators

Well, as luck would have it, I was ordered by headquarters to conduct an investigation into illegal activities at a local alligator business not two miles from my house. The investigation revealed numerous violations as well as new repercussions. As we began our investigation on September 10, 1991, Major Boots, from Baton Rouge headquarters, wanted in the limelight of the case due to potential media coverage. However, when the department learned their friend, acquitted district attorney, was the business owner's attorney, they played Pontius Pilate with me and led me to a feast for the wolves.

The first thing on the agenda for acquitted district attorney was to file a civil rights violation against me. This frivolous action placed me under an FBI microscope for nine months. Once again, I was like a leper with the department. Major Boots (alligator) said he was out. It was my case, even though he was the commanding officer at the scene calling all the shots on September 10, 1991. Major Boots's vision of positive media was outweighed by the vindictiveness of acquitted district attorney. Captain Flip and Flop, also part of the investigation, went into hiding. Captain Flip and Flop did not want to compromise one of his hunting places, the controversial camp of acquitted district attorney.

After all was said and done, the alligator case went to a jury trial. Jury trials were very uncommon in wildlife cases. Usually, these cases are held before a judge alone, but the defense can waive the district judge and be tried by jury. This tactic backfired, and the defendant was found guilty on all counts by a jury of his peers. Guilt beyond a reasonable doubt was required by all jury members, which signified the strength of the evidence presented in the trial.

The party was just beginning with acquitted district attorney when, simultaneously, he filed an appeal in the case followed by a lawsuit. Through the great grapevine, it was revealed that my house was in jeopardy. However, state statutes would indemnify me if it was determined I acted in good faith. No one wanted to challenge me on that issue. In the end, the ignoble state allegedly settled the suit for hundreds of thousands of dollars, even though the defendant was found guilty at a jury trial. The civil rights investigation continued for months after the trial, ending with a letter from the FBI, stating they found no civil rights violation had occurred.

On the heels of that investigation, Captain Flip and Flop called me on September 21, 1991, about an alligator case involving the sheriff of assumption parish's brother. The case involved untagged alligator meat. The captain ordered me not to donate the alligator meat, which was procedure. On September 22, 1991, Captain Flip and Flop called again saying the sheriff was very upset and demanded

I not file the charges. The old adage "you know who I am" slipped past my ears constantly. I usually responded to the question with a similar one, "You know who I am?" As usual, I ignored the demand not to file charges. I had to be exceptionally careful while traveling through Assumption Parish as I was on their hit list.

On September 23, 1991, the delay tactics in the indicted Ferret case came to an end. Oh, yes, this old case still existed without disposition. There were pretrial motions heard in court. It was as if the longer one delayed court action, the better the deal. In Ferret's case, that gamble paid off. The case was set for trial at a later date no less.

Day after day, year after year, nothing but controversy. This can't be fact, has to be fiction. If this was fiction, I needed to wake up because I had been in a sleeping nightmare for twenty-seven years. Lots of people said just give up. It's not worth it. Just as I was about to cave in, I would receive a phone call, which I called a message from above.

One night after an all-day grueling patrol, a lady called in a very low sincere voice asking for my help. The desperate lady stated, "Mr. Chauvin, I am sitting at my table with one can of pork and beans. I am looking at five children across the table. We have a candle for light. Our electricity was turned off today. I live down the bayou, and I am watching all these boats leave to go shrimping in closed season. My husband and I are Christian. My husband is not a violator because he feels that would be stealing from all those fishermen who wait for the open season. My husband considers this a sin, and he doesn't want to go to hell. Can you please help me?"

This was an actual phone call that inspired me for years. When I would get down, I often heard her plea for help.

The Deposition US Federal Grand Jury

Enough digressing, getting back to the real world. On September 24, 1991, I led a large group of agents outside my district on yet another alligator investigation. The lieutenant of this area was very apprehensive as we approached a large warehouse near the New Orleans International Airport. The warehouse was a shipping station for a large alligator company. During the investigation, the battery of the agents seized 390 alligator skins for various violations. Since these hides were being shipped overseas, the case was targeted by the feds. On October 23, 1991, I presented the case to Assistant US Attorney Spencer Eig, who, after months, presented the bulky case to a federal grand jury. The case now was assisted by federal agents of the US Fish and Wildlife Service. The investigation took us around the world and seemed to be centered in Singapore, China.

In an unprecedented move, the alligator company hired a prestigious law firm out of New Orleans. Their plan was to circumvent the federal grand jury proceedings by hastily filing a lawsuit against me and the Department of Wildlife and Fisheries for allegedly six million dollars.

Typical lawsuits involved depositions during which one exposes all the evidence in the case through sworn testimony that could be used in a court proceeding. The depositions for the defense were conducted by three young super aggressive yuppie attorneys. I was also under subpoena by the federal grand jury, which complicated my answering questions in a civil disposition. Assistant United States Attorney Spencer Eig instructed me to invoke a special grand jury rule (6E) not to divulge my testimony discovered in the grand jury proceedings.

Every question presented by the yuppies, I invoked the rule and did not answer. The attorneys became livid. In order to flex their muscles, the lead attorney called the federal district judge handling the case, getting him off the bench to order me to answer their questions. I spoke to the federal judge by phone. The federal judge ordered me to answer the questions, or I could be held in contempt of court. I told the judge I did not think I could divulge grand jury information in a deposition. The cocky lawyers smiled at the judge's decision.

Once off the phone, I called Assistant US Attorney Spencer Eig and asked for his input. Spencer stated I had two options: not answer the civil disposition and possibly be held in civil contempt, or answer the questions and possibly be held in criminal contempt by the grand jury rules.

Lovely, it became my choice on which contempt I preferred, both included jail. I felt criminal contempt was more serious than civil contempt. Honestly, I just did not want to submit to the yuppies' demands. I am sure it was costing hundreds of dollars per hour for their time.

The three lawyers bombarded me for hours building their case of civil contempt. Arrogantly, at one point, the yuppies asked if I knew my name, laughing. I continued to invoke the federal grand jury rules. For some reason, the lawyers asked a stupid question, which they did not know the answer. I could see they were frustrated and had taken their best shot with the federal judge.

The question asked, "What was not covered by the grand jury rules?" For one hour, I went over the 390 hides and the specific violations for each. The yuppies immediately objected. My attorney, TJ, stated, "You asked. Now he will answer." The yuppies put their face in their hands as I overwhelmed them with testimony, which they did not want on record.

Consequently, there were no grounds for civil contempt, nor any grounds for criminal contempt. TJ said, "After being browbeaten for hours, you were setting the yuppies up all along." After my lengthy answer to their one question, the yuppie attorneys gave up, terminating the deposition.

This alligator case involved the executive assistant of a United States Senator eliciting, once again, an FBI investigation into my personal life. No one wanted to push me too hard due to my reputation of going to the media and exposing the corrupt. A year or so went by, Assistant US Attorney Spencer Eig transferred to Florida. The case simply vanished into thin air as if it was a part of a Houdini act. I never found out what happened to the case. As I was bombarded by the yuppies, something caught my eye that I thought was strange. The ponytailed defendant was reading a book entitled *The Iliad and the Odyssey*, thus, giving credence to their arrogance.

Meanwhile, back at the ranch, from October 4 through October 11, 1991, I opened up the proverbial can of worms by enforcing the undersized shrimp law on the major dealers in my area. A total of thirteen dealers were charged with thousands of pounds of undersized shrimp. The shrimpers were easy targets, but in order to stop the problem, you have to stop the dealers, kind of like the war on drugs.

The shrimp count law was in place to allow small shrimp to become larger in order to have a better market. However, wildlife laws and money don't mix. It is guaranteed money will win out. My area was the exception. Trucks carrying small shrimp would not even travel through my area in fear that the illegal shrimp would be seized. This decision was worth hundreds of thousands of dollars, so the pressure was intense. Dealers called me to their places and begged me not to enforce the law; however, fishermen wanted enforcement claiming the dealers would pay low prices citing small shrimp, while the dealers found a demand and good prices. The fishermen cried foul, saying it wasn't fair. Had the prices of small shrimp been equitable, the fishermen would never have complained to me, forcing my hand.

In an unrelated matter, Colonel Cook called me stating I had no case on an alligator dealer. Colonel Cook wanted me to drop the charges. Predictably, I ignored his orders to fix, yet another, ticket.

On December 31, 1991, I was called to Baton Rouge headquarters for another alligator meeting. This meeting turned out to be a thrashing of Roy Chauvin by alligator biologists while enforcement supervisors sat back in their alligator boots and let it happen. I could tell we were getting closer to a governor's election.

Death of Senator BB

In a sad note, on September 26, 1991, my adversary, Senator BB, died of cancer. Although he had fought me for years, I honestly felt sorrow in his passing. I had forgiven his transgressions over the years and hoped he did not carry his animosity to the grave.

His son took over the senator's job but was completely different from his father. No threats, just cooperation came from him throughout the rest of my career. His brother took over the senator's seat after his brother's term expired. They truly had a dynasty, even though their father was misguided at times.

CHAPTER 21

Déjà Vu

Return of Governor Rico

Well, just as the old administration within the department had predicted, Governor Rico came back into power. Governor Rico seemed to rub the corruption in the faces of the ignorant people, and they loved it. Strong and committed, the people portrayed a sense of the following of Jim Jones. Although misled, they surrendered their souls and consciousness for the sake of a miscreant dictator.

I knew it wouldn't take long for the old administration to blow the dust off the old practices and dismantle the advances, although slight, that had been accomplished. For the first time in my career, I became thoroughly disgusted; however, I had two years until retirement. A similar situation that US Magistrate Egret faced. That disgust didn't last long because that would have been the end of me. I decided to embrace the end of my career wide open, somewhat like a kamikaze pilot. I began a physical regimen to get my cardiovascular system in tip-top shape in order to brace for the fourth round of war.

On January 16, 1992, Colonel Cook called about complaints pertaining to the Grand Isle shrimp line. I ignored everything, waiting for repercussions.

My supporters were at an all-time low with the reelection of Governor Rico, so I decided to lay low waiting for the corrupt administration to reload my gun with evidence.

The new secretary of the Department of Wildlife and Fisheries was a longtime employee who rose through the ranks during the Rico Administration. It didn't take long, on February 3, 1992, new Secretary Fish, fresh off his victory, called me to Baton Rouge headquarters to read me the riot act as it pertained to alligators. It seems that everyone wanted a shot to put me in my place. At times, I felt the corrupt had a bounty on my head. My tactic at this point was "in one ear and out the other." I refused to prostitute my convictions so late in the game. Bring it on, Jack.

Secretary Fish: Cronies and Gators

On February 26, 1992, I was ordered by Colonel Cook to attend an alligator meeting in Baton Rouge. The refuge division, in charge of the alligator program, refused to let me in their offices. I thought their efforts were childish and somewhat comical. Is that all you have? The refuge division stated anybody but Roy Chauvin can attend the meeting. I asked Secretary Fish what he wanted me to do. He sided with his crony biologists. This set the tone for the Rico Administration.

On February 28, 1992, again, I was asked to go down the yellow brick road leading to the alligator biologists. There was yet another alligator meeting I was not allowed to attend. During their meeting, I went to McDonald's and got a Happy Meal.

Then on March 24, 1992, I did get to attend an alligator meeting along with Captain Flip and Flop and Major Boots (alligator). My opinions were not relevant. Do as you are told. That philosophy never sat well with me.

On March 27, 1992, while on assignment in Grand Isle, we seized a seven-thousand-pound truckload of king mackerel. The people in Grand Isle didn't like it. Immediately, I was on the removal list at Grand Isle—again.

On March 31, 1992, there was another alligator meeting in Baton Rouge headquarters. I called the meeting The Showdown, which reared its ugly head once again and was prophetic of things to come. All the big empty guns were present, including, but not limited to, department lawyers Spirit of the Law and Go Along, head staff alligator biologists, Deputy Secretary Leave Alone, Major Boots, Captain Flip and Flop, Colonel Cook, Lieutenant Colonel Silver Tongue, and the only one of my side, Contract Attorney TJ.

TJ stated the state's position in the gator lawsuits had been compromised by gator biologists meeting with and giving information to parties suing the state. TJ stated this action constituted nothing less than an ethics violation. I felt TJ was blowing the wrong horn. This administration had no ethics. Ethic's laws rolled off their backs, like water rolls off the back of a duck.

Secretary Fish, embellished by a lack of wisdom, stated strict enforcement was driving people away. What he meant to say was "Let's go back to selective enforcement."

On April 1, 1992, appropriately called April Fool's Day, the department made a deal with the company that was under the scrutiny of a federal grand jury. The department and court agreed to terms of a worthless injunction on the company for illegal markings and tied on alligator tags. This gutted the entire case. The 396 hides seized in the raid would not be affected. This was a total sellout by the department.

Alligator tags were placed on alligators immediately upon taking. The tags were numbered to track the origin of the gator and to prevent abuse. The tags were locked in place to preserve the integrity of the program. Also, each year, the alligator hunters had to skin the gators, leaving a permanent identifying mark, such as a flap of skin in a particular area on the skin. This was to distinguish legal hides from illegal ones. Without strict enforcement, the program was a bust.

On April 29, 1991, former-acquitted district attorney represented a defendant who was charged during the roadblock operation in which the National Geographic Society had filmed. The former district attorney tried to get the evidence suppressed (thrown out) in a motion in court. He was unsuccessful. He just wanted to let me know that he didn't forget about me.

On May 7 and 8, 1992, in two separate raids at Grand Isle and Belle Pass, respectively, a total of thirty closed-season shrimp cases were investigated. The politicians aimed their guns at me but never pulled the trigger, fearing repercussions.

The lack of retaliation signified Governor Rico was still pondering the blank federal subpoena from John Voltz with a stern warning. Sneaky pressure rather than wide open was the order of the day.

On Thursday, May 12, 1992, fourteen more closed-season shrimp cases were made in the same area. I was definitely pushing their buttons, but there was no response. One must remember the leader of the pack was Senator Blood Brother who was no longer a factor. No one wanted to step up and wave the illicit banner.

On June 5, 1992, I had a meeting with the new District Attorney of Lafourche Parish. He previously stated I wasn't his favorite person. District Attorney took the opportunity to let me know he would not allow me to threaten him, like I treated acquitted district attorney of Terrebonne Parish. District Attorney stated he would come after me before I got started. In one ear, out the other.

Thinking The Iliad and Odyssey gator case faded away like smoke in the wind, on June 16, 1992, there was a motion "to compel me" to testify at deposition in federal court. The motion to compel failed in federal court. So my stand on invoking the federal grand jury rule was upheld in federal court. That did not stop the yuppies. On June 17, 1992, the yuppies filed a motion to compel me to be deposed with a state Judge in Baton Rouge. Again, the yuppies were not successful. I remained firm on invoking the federal grand jury rules.

Then on June 30, 1992, the United States attorney's office dismissed the indictment against Iliad and Odyssey Gator Company without prejudice. Legally meaning that the case could never come up again. The alleged dismissal was due to the Speedy Trial Act. The US attorney was not ready to proceed, therefore, dismissed. If the case had been dismissed with prejudice, the case could have been resurrected.

After the decision, I spoke to LK of the United States attorney's office, who disgustingly said politics often dictate action. He did not expand on that statement, fearing repercussions, but I knew what it meant.

On July 1, 1992, in a federal hearing to justify the fix on the Iliad and Odyssey alligator case, the federal judge ruled that Assistant United States Attorney Spencer Eig was present at the prior deposition against rules. If memory serves me right, Spencer Eig, by phone, interrupted grand jury rules of secrecy. That was it.

Complaint Filed with US Inspector General

On July 2, 1992, I cried foul. I filed an official complaint with the United States office of Inspector General, whose job was to investigate improprieties by government officials and employees. I cited my dilemma of testimony in a civil case versus divulging information by a federal grand jury in a criminal investigation. In defense of AUSA Spencer Eig, I only asked about the rules of the federal grand jury prohibiting my deposition.

On July 6, 1992, at 4:20 p.m., Colonel Cook said Secretary Fish told him I was causing trouble in Washington, D.C.

Also on July 6, I was called by the senior resident federal agent Jim Bartee of the US Fish and Wildlife Service, saying he received a call from a high-level official in Washington, D.C. The official wanted Jim Bartee to get me to "cool it." I knew I had pressed the right buttons with the responses. I did not withdraw my complaint.

During the Iliad and Odyssey alligator investigation, a United States senator and especially an executive assistant to the senator were mentioned during the investigation. The executive assistant was up to his ears in the investigation.

I learned early on that you don't make an allegation unless you have proof of that allegation and more. To submit part of an allegation places the target on notice. Deep down, only you and the target know the truth. Playing on that assumption, the investigator can extract far more than he already knows. This maneuver also prohibits open confrontation during the investigation in fear of revealing more accusations. It is just a giant game with serious consequences.

On July 15, 1992, I was called to yet another meeting with Colonel Cook and Deputy Secretary Leave Alone, who said Secretary Fish was talking bad about me. I was nothing but trouble. In a new twist, Secretary Fish was supposed to air out my actions before the next Louisiana Department of Wildlife and Fisheries monthly commission meeting filled with appointees of Governor Rico. For the commission to take my actions as an agenda item was totally inappropriate. The commission had no authority, or jurisdiction in dealing with me. Only civil service could act on factual information. Secretary Fish wanted to air his complaints about me through a novel source. Every one of the commission members knew me anyway, so my disrupting the apple cart wasn't new. In fact, the commission probably did not want to have anything to do with me, not out of respect but fear. What's new?

Colonel Cook said his testimony at the commission meeting stated I was a good agent, always top five in production and statewide agent of the year twice. Talk about falling on deaf ears. Colonel Cook stated Secretary Fish wanted my personnel file, which I heard filled the back of a pickup truck, but the colonel said he had purged the file before he gave it to Secretary Fish. This was done in order to remove self-incriminating information.

All this hoopla indicated the colonel and Deputy Secretary Leave Alone, who was a direct liaison to Governor Rico, had ulterior motives. Good politicians can stab you in the back and make you love it, but I wasn't fooled. Washington really had them upset.

On July 23, 1992, Captain Flip and Flop called me to say Colonel Cook was going after me due to the complaint to the office of Inspector General in Washington, D.C. This was a self-serving proclamation for Captain Flip and Flop, appropriately named. Captain Flip and Flop saw no better way to air his anger at Colonel Cook than to have Roy do his dirty work. Blame it on Roy, everybody else does.

Also on July 23 as the phones were buzzing over the OG's investigation, I got yet another call. Federal Agent John Collins, who collaborated and co-authored the Iliad and Odyssey gator investigation, stated his boss in Atlanta, Georgia, was trying to distance himself from the case due to the questioning effort of the office of inspector general. My complaint seemed to rattle the cages of anyone who knew about the investigation.

On August 19, 1992, there was another meaningless alligator meeting. How did anyone get anything done by calling all these meetings, which accomplished nothing? In attendance was the secretary, deputy secretary, the entire hierarchy of the refuge division, department attorney, colonel, captain, lieutenant colonel, and major. My entourage was pretty impressive. I felt like I was on a merry-go-round riding the same horse over and over again. I have to give it to them. They were persistent, but I was motivated by my conviction, which they could not compete with, or twist.

The result of the meeting was that the biologists now said they could not do away with the tagging system. Tagging alligators was their only means of tracking mechanism. Maybe the office of inspector general had something to do with changing their minds. The Iliad and Odyssey case had numerous untagged alligator hides. The department attorney, Spirit of the Law, said current regulations were unenforceable. What's new?

After this meeting, Secretary Fish kept me, Deputy Secretary Leave Alone, and Captain Flip and Flop to discuss the Wildlife Agent's Association's written response to Secretary Fish's complaint about me to the office of inspector general in Washington. The association, unknowing to me, demanded protection and noninterference in enforcement matters.

This stand by the association was not just to back me but, rather, a calculated move by Colonel Cook. The enforcement division was losing its stroke in the department due to the appointment of Secretary Fish, a longtime biologist in the department. Secretary Fish took the side of the biologists in any action. Secretary Fish said the Iliad and Odyssey case had become personal between me and chief alligator biologist, Rock Along. Secretary Fish said taxpayers in Louisiana were losing money due to the fight. The meeting was worthless, not offering solutions.

After the meeting, Deputy Secretary said he wrote a letter of reprimand on Biologist Rock Along, but nothing was done.

It's amazing how one little letter objecting to corruption and seeking justice can cause such a stir. If only the Department of Wildlife and Fisheries had concentrated on wildlife as much as they concentrated on me, we would have had speckled trout (popular game fish) swimming in everyone's bathtub due to overpopulation and great management. This analogy applied to all wildlife and its management. These timeless meetings accomplished nothing but, rather, were an attempt to vindictively cast judgment on me, which absolutely had no effect on the way I approached my job. I worked for the good people and the little animals who didn't have a say in this ridiculous facade portrayed by a meaningless and misguided state agency funded by the public known as the Department of Wildlife and Fisheries. Oh! Too much on my soapbox.

Meeting with Deputy Secretary

On November 19, 1992, the gill net problem still flourished in my area. Not a single gill net went undetected without my knowledge due to a network of informants and public observation. The gill net issue was still a hot and volatile issue. On this day, we made several gill net cases in which the violators would not cooperate. In fact, the violators interfered with the investigation resulting in the subject's arrest. After a lengthy daylong investigation, I received a call to meet with Deputy Secretary Leave Alone. The meeting was from 3 p.m. to 7 p.m. discussing my actions concerning gill nets and the arrest. Deputy Secretary Leave Alone, appropriately named, offered no directions, or suggestions. However, I was smart enough to know the meeting was a silent warning, not just a friendly conversation.

CHAPTER 22

1993 SOS

Article 1970s

1993 started off with little fanfare. By that, I mean I was not bombarded with controversial meetings, or events. The work of wildlife enforcement took priority during these times, which would inevitably set up another battle. It was a time for me to regroup and reflect.

The Rico Administration would go to great lengths to satisfy their friends and circumvent the law. During my research, I found an old newspaper article from the 1970s. The title of the article was "Jimmy Resigns after Raid on Dear Friends of the Governor." Jimmy was the chief of enforcement of LDWF. According to the article, the enforcement division raided A Fish Market. Part owner was one of governor's chief financial backers. The case involved the selling of crappie, a popular game fish. Jimmy stated, "If I am going to be called on the carpet because I send my people to enforce the law, then I am not going to be a part of it at all." Jimmy said that the governor told him he had embarrassed his dear friends. Jimmy said what capped it off was when the governor told the media that he instructed Jimmy to enforce the law. He resigned after the incident.

This article exemplified the tactics of the Rico Administration. Under the table, criticize your efforts to do your job to the point of resigning but on the surface, enforce the law. The prolific hypocrisy of the Rico Administration seems to touch everyone in the administration. The hierarchy of the LDWF used these tactics but without the legal finesse of Governor Rico, their idol. They took it too far and got into trouble.

Fish Farms

The protection of friends developed in lower Lafourche Parish under the guise of fish farms. Gill nets were illegal in this area, but a marshland owner could set up a fish farm. These operations were set up in the estuaries where fish migrated.

Prized redfish were targeted by fish farms. This process sanctioned by the LDWF created an enforcement nightmare. The operation fell under the jurisdiction of fish biologist Weenie, who caved in to the demands at the drop of a hat. According to Major Boots, Chief Biologist Ferret would be in charge of shipping redfish. Major Boots said this practice was very unusual for Biologist Ferret to be involved at that level.

On March 17, 1993, I had a meeting with District Attorney. The meetings were never productive. Usually, the sole purpose was criticism. District Attorney called me into his office on the most trivial of matters. It was as though he wanted to keep me under his thumb with these reminders. He was playing big league ball with a little league bat. I just flipped the gnat off my ear.

The gill net issue flourished once again due to Governor Rico policies. The LDWF department attorney, Spirit of the Law, instructed me to go by the spirit of the law. Vague and inconsistent policies proved to be an embarrassing disaster in the public's eyes and the court.

Then, once again, I became the victim of the waste of time meetings at headquarters in Baton Rouge. I would be ordered to attend the Louisiana Department of Wildlife and Fisheries commission meetings. I just stood there—no input, or questions asked of me, listening to the chaos of the Rico Administration appointees.

March 24, 1993, there was a change in who would attend the crab task force meetings. Major Boots would be there to reflect the department's wishes. The problem was undersized crabs flourished once again. Captain Flip and Flop was infuriated by the department's decision. Captain Flip and Flop stated Major Boots had his own commercial crab operation on the side—conflict of interest, fox in the henhouse, you be the judge.

As if on cue, April 1, 1993, District Attorney called me into his office over several undersized crab cases. His rhetoric was always the same: I was too hard on the fishermen. There was never any mention there was a violation of the law. The DA had the sole authority to drop the charges; however, that would subject him to the criticism of those who wanted the law enforced. The DA chose to try to intimidate me into his web of deceit. In essence, he wanted his cake and to eat it too.

Strike Force Misbehaving

On April 7, 1993, the staff of the enforcement division held a meeting in Grand Isle, Louisiana. Those in attendance were Colonel Cook, Major Gopher, Captain Flip and Flop, Captain Opportunist, me, and the newly created statewide task force. Properly managed and trained this task force was a great idea; however, these hired guns would sweep into an area directed by headquarters wreaking havoc. Their lack of knowledge of the laws and reckless attitude was not professional.

They had no respect for me, or my knowledge of the workings of my district. At one point, I had a young trainee task force member tell me in a crowd that he did not work for me. I wrote him up for disciplinary action. Instead, he got a promotion.

If the cases of the taskforce lacked merit, or selective enforcement, I refused to notarize, or sign off on their reports always with written justification. This created chaos among the entire enforcement staff, who could have overridden my reasons and notarized the citations. The public demanded consistent interpretation of the law, which was not in purview of the task force due to the fact they received their direction from Rico headquarters.

To give you an example of the kind of agents who made up the task force, late one night, a radio transmission stated a task force agent had been shot at as he sat in his truck on the side of the road. The truck had been hit with several shots; however, the agent was not injured. There were questions about the shooting from the very beginning. Things did not add up. Headquarters became very hush-hush about the shooting because the agent was a favored one. After a very short investigation, it was discovered the agent, seeking attention, shot his own truck. These guys were totally out of control and lacked direction. The enforcement division secretly placed the agent on some kind of leave. The agent just seemed to vanish in thin air. I had objected to the department on some of the agent's unscrupulous tactics, but nothing was done.

In another incident with the task force, on May 10, 1993, Major Gopher who was in charge of the task force and seaplane called me late at night, stating he wanted me back in the seaplane. I had been banned from the plane due to my productivity. Now the reversal: The seaplane would be under my supervision. I questioned the urgency of the change and was informed that the pilot and task force agent were caught fishing from the plane behind a locked gate in my area of Lafourche Parish. The property owner who caught the agents was very upset and a "dear friend" of Governor Rico. To straighten up the mess, I was placed in charge but not for long.

On June 16, 1993, I spoke to the Rotary Club of Houma, Louisiana. Questions always were directed toward my conflicts with the Rico Administration. Most of the people were supporters. The department tried to regulate my attendance at such meetings to no avail. The department feared repercussions.

On June 28, 1993, I became aware that the district attorney in Terrebonne Parish considered calling a grand jury on the alligator mess due to the testimony of Biologist Rock Along and his selective regulations. The tenacity of the district attorney began to fade. He seemed to be frustrated, and I think he contemplated giving up. My father always said, "You can give out but never give up."

I always seemed to have a fly on the wall in the secret meetings in Baton Rouge headquarters. On July 28, 1993, Federal Agent Jim Bartee said he received a call from Colonel Cook. Colonel Cook had attended a meeting with Secretary Fish, Deputy Secretary Leave

Alone, and Rico Administration Caribou. Caribou started the meeting, according to Colonel Cook, shouting, "Roy should be fired." They were so misguided that Caribou had called the meeting without checking the facts. Caribou had received the wrong information and hastily called the meeting in hopes of taking me down. As it turned out, right after the meeting, the vain group learned that the culprit was another lieutenant in another district. In the heat of the moment, it was Roy, go figure.

The reason Colonel Cook called my friend Jim Bartee was to deflect any blame by me on him. Colonel Cook portrayed the "I didn't have anything to do with it" attitude, fearing my written counter-attack especially when it wasn't me.

On August 3, 1993, in Hammond, Louisiana, there was a big meeting on the Iliad and Odyssey alligator case at TJ's law office. I was so sick of this case. They had to address some sort of motion in court pertaining to the civil case.

Captain Flip and Flop False Arrest

On August 4, 1993, I had to go to Baton Rouge to testify in a fisherman's lawsuit for false arrest. It was difficult to testify on the department's behalf due to the fact that the fisherman was correct in this case. The incompetence of Captain Flip and Flop shone brightly during this set of embarrassing and dangerous circumstances. Also, Captain Flip and Flop was a hothead who was never wrong. Even if knowingly wrong, he would not back down. His pride was more important than the truth. I had to deal with this ego trip constantly throughout my career. He was an obstacle to professionalism and easy to control by headquarters.

During a closed shrimp season flight, I was having trouble with a number of boats trawling in closed waters. We were escorting a number of boats into the dock for seizure. I was circling the plane over the violating vessels waiting for agents to assist by boat. There was a great deal of talk on the radio to make sure the agents boarded the correct boats. The shrimp had concentrated in one specific area, and there was chaos among numerous boats. Once they saw the plane, the boats all began to head toward open waters in a mass exit. I would concentrate on the vessels farthest inside the closed area, identifying the violators by vessel name. It took a great deal of communication not to confuse vessels. Captain Flip and Flop was listening to my radio communications and decided to drive forty miles away to assist.

Captain Flip and Flop, in his haste to arrest someone, got the names of the boats confused and arrested the crewmembers of the wrong boat at an extremely hostile dock. The owner of the dock, a former LDWF commission member, became very upset. Of course, when my name was mentioned as seeing the boat from the plane, it only added fuel to the fire. There were numerous fishermen at the dock defending Captain Flip and Flop's target. Without calling me to verify the boat's name as one of my targets, Captain Flip and Flop arrested everyone on the boat. Captain Flip and Flop's pride got in the way of sound judgment. The lieutenant with Captain Flip and Flop tried to tell him to slow down and wait for my verification, but now, Captain Flip and Flop was mad. When fishermen were correct, they would fight you. The large crowd became more and more upset. The lieutenant called me and stated I needed to get to the dock right away. As I arrived at the noisy hostile dock, Captain Flip and Flop single-handedly arrested everyone on the innocent vessel, including a subject who was in a wheelchair. This action by Captain Flip and Flop handcuffing everyone and arresting the handicapped individual was too much for the fishermen to bear. Captain Flip and Flop was in a shouting match with the captain of the boat. I immediately informed Captain Flip and Flop that he had the wrong boat. He screamed at me saying I had called that boat as a violation. Then he turned his anger on me because I would not back him up even though he was wrong. I told the captain to get in his car and leave before a physical confrontation occurred. The lieutenant had to escort the belligerent captain to his car. I tried to calm the situation down, but the fishermen would have nothing to do with it. I told the captain of the vessel that no one would be charged. The captain said they were falsely arrested and placed in handcuffs. The icing on the cake was the carrying of the wheelchair victim off the boat to secure his arrest. I agreed with their assessment of the situation. I would never have charged the handicapped person, much less arrested him in his wheelchair. I barely got off the dock without a physical fight. The captain of the vessel sued and won.

Captain Flip and Flop in his narrow-minded assessment of the situation blamed the other lieutenant and me for the disaster. The captain also convinced headquarters that we were wrong and not him. The captain said the lieutenant and I did not back him. The captain said we should have agreed with his arrest—in essence, lie for him. The ignoble cult of law enforcement officers covering up the wrongdoing of a fellow officer.

Following on the heels of the arrest debacle came my yearly civil service rating. Captain Flip and Flop singled out the arrest incident and his displeasure in the results, giving me a horrible civil service rating. His narrow-mindedness was impossible to deal with. He was never wrong.

At this time, I had twenty years of service and was eligible for retirement. I was working on an exit strategy. I had never taken a day of sick leave in twenty years, nor had I used much annual leave. I wanted to fade away and take a little well-deserved leave to spend with my wife and eight foster children. I had three years of accumulated leave. I spoke to Captain Flip and Flop about my plans, and he said he had the authority to grant leave or not. This power trip was used to keep control over me. This act was more personal than department oriented. Captain Flip and Flop stated he could work me seven days a week, and there was nothing I could do about it. This decision led to a very serious legal problem for the department spearheaded by me with the backing of the fair labor standards act, as you shall see.

The year ended with constant controversies. I probably attended more staff meetings in Baton Rouge than ever before. I almost believed the department collectively set their calendars to certain dates in advance in which I would be called to a meeting. It was getting very old and tiring. However, I could not show weakness. I had to fake it saying to controversy, "Let's get it on." This arrogant tactic seemed to intimidate some, but there was always a newcomer in the wings waiting to take their shot.

CHAPTER 23

Should I Stay, or Should I Go?

1994 was a pivotal time in my career. I was eligible to retire even though I was forty-three years old. I pondered the thought of going back to law school, or even becoming a schoolteacher, but I realized that my job was not over. Maybe I was too proud to admit defeat. Should I continue the fight, or should I retire and just fade away like the old soldier who never dies. My fast-paced life had caught up with me asking myself the proverbial question, "Is that all there is?" I had two jobs—the Louisiana Department of Wildlife and Fisheries and raising foster children, both with special needs and demands.

It was the middle of the fourth term of the Rico Administration, and no one seemed to care. The thousands of pages of numerous lawsuits were consuming all my time. I felt like I was a civil attorney rather than a wildlife agent. The light at the end of the tunnel of hope was going dim. I rationalized my decision to stay by imposing this philosophy: Life is a gift. You can always look around and see other people with more serious troubles than yourself, yet they persevere. Exploit all your talents and attributes so that in the winter of your life, you don't look back and say, "I could have done more." I took a deep breath of life and decided to fight longer. Maybe I did not heed the warning, maybe my pride got in the way of rational thinking.

The Shooting

After all this contemplating, could things get worse? One of the most horrifying events to come was on the early morning horizon of January 7, 1994. Nothing in law enforcement is ever routine, and to treat your environment in such a manner could be deadly. On this night patrol of January 7, 1994, the cold reality of my job surfaced, confronting death face to face with the grim reaper looking to grab your hand.

On this very cold and dreary night, Agent Gary Benoit and I were on patrol in Lafourche Parish. Like many patrols before, we spotted a light in a field along a wood line. This area had a good deer population, and many people chose to hunt illegally at night.

As our investigation unfolded, we discovered a shell road next to a house that seemed to be our way to the potential violator. We were in a marked truck in full uniform. As we crept in darkness to avoid detection, the subject continued to shine his light randomly in the field out of the driver's side window. As we approached head on at a snail's pace in the dark, our distance was closing in on the subject. As a subject's headlight illuminated our vehicle, he turned his lights out. Simultaneously, we turned our lights on. The vehicles were approximately twenty feet apart. As we crept, three shots rang out from the truck. Agent Benoit thought we had picked up barbed wire in the drive shaft of the truck. I shouted, "He's shooting." I managed to open my door and began identifying myself as a game warden. I drew my weapon and aimed it in the direction of the lone subject, continually identifying myself. When I opened my door, the light illuminated the inside of our truck as the subject remained in the dark. I glanced over to Agent Benoit who was struggling to get his seat belt off.

The subject exited the truck with his assault rifle aimed at the windshield and shot two more times over the top of the truck. The muzzled blast lit up the night sky. I continued to identify myself, not sure if his intentions were to intimidate us, or kill one of us. You role-play these situations in training, but the real thing is a lot more intense and fast.

Now, after the second volley of shots, I could just see the top of the head of the subject as he carefully rested the weapon, identified as a multishot assault weapon on the door of the truck taking close aim at the struggling Agent Benoit's chest. I knew the subject had twenty-five more rounds in the gun, so I had to carefully plan my shot. For the first time in my career, I began squeezing the trigger on my weapon with the intention of stopping the assault with one shot. All of a sudden, in a split second, the subject looked at his gun and disappeared behind the door. As I waited for him to reappear, with the intention of shooting, Agent Benoit flashed in my line of fire, running around the door at the crouched subject as he attempted to reload. Agent Benoit tackled the subject as I held my gun on him. As it turned out, the subject had pulled the trigger for a third volley of shots, and the gun jammed. He disappeared for cover to reload.

My heart was racing. My mind was trying to comprehend what had just happened. Flashing through my mind during this ordeal was the possibility that I might die in a muddy sugarcane field. I actually envisioned myself lying there dying.

The mind works very fast in such intense situations. This was the most horrible feeling that I had ever had. I always said I would have to be shot to fire back. I nearly killed someone.

Agents from throughout the area came to our assistance. The violator had been drinking, not drunk, and was not the least bit apologetic. He showed no remorse saying, "I should have killed y'all."

He stated he knew we were game wardens and didn't care. As it turned out, he had planned his ambush. As we passed the house at the beginning of the shell road, we triggered a silent alarm system, informing someone in the house of our presence. According to the subject, he was called when we went through the gate to warn him that we were coming.

The subject was prepared for a war with all his weapons. The violator had a fully loaded sawed-off shotgun with five rounds of buckshot, the assault weapon with twenty-four more rounds in the clip, and a fully loaded pistol. Agent Benoit remained calm, but I was very upset over the events. The subject stated we were trespassing, and he had a right to take action. He never shut up, informing us of his political clout in Lafourche Parish. I turned the investigation over to the assisting agents. I could not take the violator's mouthing off anymore.

The formal charges filed in conjunction with this incident were as follows:

1) two counts aggravated assault on a police officer
2) one count of resisting arrest
3) two counts of public intimidation
4) one count possession of stolen gun
5) one count hunting deer at night
6) one count hunting from moving vehicle
7) one count disturbing the peace by intoxication

All these charges were filed in Lafourche Parish.

As it turned out, the subject had political ties. His father was a popular politician and former mayor of Thibodaux, Louisiana. Also during investigation, we learned the property allegedly belonged to Tulane University in New Orleans.

In a very strange twist, it was discovered by tracking the serial numbers on the pistol that this same pistol had been stolen from the evidence locker at the Houma City Police Department. The gun was evidence in a case involving an armed robbery in Houma. Not to my surprise, the mysterious circumstances surrounding that gun remains a mystery to this day.

The only person who called to inquire about the incident was Captain Flip and Flop who had to report to Baton Rouge headquarters. It was clear we were on our own with the shooting. Colonel Cook should have been leading the charge defending his agents against such situations, but after all, his name was Colonel Cook.

National Rifle Association

The following week, without a response from the department, Colonel Cook called me. Colonel Cook stated there was an attorney in his office that would like to talk to me about the shooting. The attorney assured me he did not represent the defendant.

The attorney began by stating the offense report revealed an assault weapon was used in the incident. Must have been a "dear friend" of Rico to give him my offense report. The attorney stated he represented the National Rifle Association, looking into every case involving the controversial weapon. The attorney had the audacity to ask me if there was anything that could be done about the charges involving the assault weapon.

I asked the attorney if anyone had ever shot at him. He stated, "No." I told the attorney he might change his attitude if he came face-to-face with the muzzle blast of an assault rifle, knowing that five shots were fired and another twenty-five rounds in the clip ready to end your life. He began to plead his agenda. I became irritated at his lack of concern for the victim of an assault, stating I would pursue this case with all the pressure and vigor that I could find. I told the attorney I did not want to talk to him anymore, so he gave the phone to Colonel Cook who was listening to the conversation. The colonel chastised me for not cooperating with the attorney and for telling the attorney that I would pursue the case. I told the colonel I did not want to talk to him anymore about the case due to his lack of support.

Lack of Prosecution

I knew we had an uphill battle getting the case prosecuted in Lafourche Parish due to my relationship with the DA. To add fuel to the fire, one of my agents went to his uncle to apply pressure on the DA in the assault case. This uncle was the number one critic of the DA The uncle applied pressure by solidifying hunting clubs in the area to push for prosecution. As it turned out, the DA blamed me for the move to involve the agent's influential uncle. True to form, the department sided with the DA and had the agent answer questions from the department and the DA about who went to the agent's uncle. The agent quickly felt the heat and said I went to his uncle. The agent said he knew nothing about it.

Sometimes pressure, fear, and ambition creates liars. This same agent resigned a short time later because he could not rise through the ranks fast enough.

On March 13, 1994, Agent Benoit and I met with an assistant district attorney in Lafourche Parish to discuss the assault case. Not to my surprise, the assistant DA said we did not have an assault case, or any other case. I dramatized the case for the assistant DA stating, "What if I take my gun out right now—shoot three times over your head? Take a better aim and shoot two more times over your head, then to cap it off, take dead aim between your eyes, pull the trigger, and the gun misfires." I asked him, "How do you think you would feel?" The assistant DA said nothing.

I told the assistant DA the fact no action was taken on the case had nothing to do with the merits of the case but rather reflected the political rhetoric of his boss, DA, and his dislike for me. The assistant DA stated I had already upset the DA by having the public attack the DA for lack of action. The honest public was bewildered and infuriated by the district attorney's actions; however, the case never went to trial.

I was confronted with the reality that everyone in Lafourche Parish could take a shot at me, and nothing would be done. I didn't know how many bullets I could dodge.

I could not let the decision of the district attorney stand unanswered. The only alternative was to file a civil suit in Lafourche Parish against the defendant for aggravated assault. Here we go, another lawsuit.

After months of delays and discovery, we finally went to the deposition phase of the lawsuit. As it turned out, a state representative from New Orleans represented the defendant. Most attorneys have a condescending attitude when dealing with nonattorneys, so was the case of this attorney dealing with me. At one point during the deposition, the defense attorney called me a liar pertaining to a question of my taking sick leave. My testimony was I had not taken a day of sick leave in twenty-one years. The attorney actually stopped the deposition to make a call to verify my claim. He came from the break stating, "Most state employees take all the leave they can, but you are the exception." No apology for calling me a liar. This set the tone for the rest of my deposition. The exorbitant fees were worthless when it came to attacking me. Not many questions were asked by the defense, who soon gave up due to the brick wall I had set up during my preparation.

Rather than being embarrassed at trial, the case was settled for an undisclosed amount. The case was not about money, but rather, the decision was a substitute for a criminal conviction. The suit confirmed we had been assaulted.

Agent Benoit, my loyal friend, shortly, thereafter, resigned citing unfair politics. He told me he could not take the pressure. Not long after, Agent Gary Benoit, at fifty years old, dropped dead of a massive heart attack. The pressure was too much to take.

Agent Benoit's death was a wake-up call. The pressure of the job was taking its toll on me. I was not feeling well—very tired and losing steam. The doctors said my blood pressure was high. I was not overweight and exercised daily. I failed a stress test and was hospitalized for an angiogram. The test found nothing. The doctors, aware of my lifestyle, said stress was the only factor in my illness. The doctors literally told me to slow down, or die. This reality check was hard to take. I did not know how to back off, let things go. That was not me. This was a secret dilemma I had to deal with silently.

The bickering, the trivial lawsuits, interdepartmental politics, and cutthroat tactics continued. This reinforced my belief that after I was gone these things will be present and thrive.

CHAPTER 24

End of Governor Rico

This was the last year of the Rico Administration, so everyone put on hold their vendettas and hid their corruption a little better. Out of sight, out of mind. They did not know who would be the next governor. My motto was "anybody but Rico." Knowing fully well that politics and favors never change in the roll of the dice where your soul is the wager only serves to expose different faces but same old, same old prevails. I had had enough and started to apply for well-deserved leave. I felt with time off, I could recharge my batteries and come back wide open. Easier said than done.

New Administration: Buddy or Not

Under the new administration, my old buddy and member of the Gulf Coast Conservation Association became Secretary of the Department of Wildlife and Fisheries. I told myself, "Well, maybe I do have a last hooray in me." New governor, new ideas, so I thought as I rekindled the ray of light in the deep recesses of my mind.

I wasted no time with a list of corrupt activities that needed to be addressed. It was my thinking that the new secretary would remember the clandestine meetings that literally took place in the middle of the night to correct wrongdoings. The Gulf Coast Conservation Association's main efforts focused on the gill net issue, which had been totally quashed by my efforts and subsequent enforcement of new laws, publicity, litigation, and judicial ruling.

Well, my buddy did not need me anymore and betrayed me by siding with the ignoble regimen in the Department of Wildlife and Fisheries. I looked into Secretary Buddy's initial appointment to the wildlife and fisheries commission. To my surprise, I discovered Secretary Buddy had been initially appointed to the commission in the waning months of the Rico Administration. Should I have expected more from him other than the tactics of Governor Rico? I was faced with enduring another four years of a regimen similar to Governor Rico, which was an enormous burden. Would it ever end?

Unsatisfactory Rating for Whistleblowing

Secretary Buddy supported the chain of incompetent command within the department who chose to bash me with an unsatisfactory civil service rating. I had to counter the rating, so I filed a grievance on January 29, 1996. As usual, the prostituted convictions of the chain of command resonated. My goal was to appeal the rating, through the grievance process, with Secretary Buddy to feel out his exact agenda for the future.

Like the rest of the department, his pompous attitude was I don't have to go by the rules of civil service. Therefore, Secretary Buddy did not answer the civil service appeal within the legal time limit.

Retaliation: Drug Screens

Immediately, the department retaliated by sending me to Our Lady of the Lake Hospital in Baton Rouge for a drug screen test, not once but twice in a short period of time. The second drug screen test was not a random test, but it was targeted. Different procedures were used. I objected, citing harassment, and filed another annoying grievance on the random selection process as well as the targeted process. There was no drugs, and I won another grievance.

From March 18, 1996, through July 20, 1996, I went on sick leave. Eighty-three days of sick leave with a total of 120 days off. My doctor called it stress leave. The doctor really hoped that I would retire. All of a sudden, stress leave became an epidemic among the older agents. The older agents said, "If Roy can do it, why not us?" The department dubbed the leave "Chauvin leave."

Immediately upon my return, Captain Flip and Flop informed me I was exempt from overtime. Captain Flip and Flop stated he could work me seven days a week, denying all leave. I deferred that decision to the Human Resources director, G.T., who placed in writing that I was not exempt from the Fair Labor Standards Act. She stated I could not work overtime without compensation. I gave the letter to Captain Flip and Flop who stated Colonel Cook advised him to "throw the letter away. It doesn't apply to you."

Then I finally got to meet with Secretary Buddy, one-on-one, to discuss his goals and my grievance. He violated grievance procedure policy by not responding in a timely manner, nor at the third step of my grievance afford me a hearing. Secretary Buddy called the hearing a meeting. Secretary Buddy started the meeting by saying he already answered my grievance on my rating by upholding enforcement's findings. I reminded Secretary Buddy how he had used me in the past, and also on how he, if the opportunity presented itself, would drastically change things within the Department of Wildlife and Fisheries. I asked Secretary Buddy if all his past assertions were just rhetoric. I told him it was a shame that now he has the opportunity to change things, but his path was nothing more than the Rico wishes of the past. I told Secretary Buddy one of the issues I was condemned for in my grievance pertaining to influence from outside parties was a direct result of him and his coconspirators to bring down the corrupt practices of the Rico Administration as they pertained to Wildlife enforcement. "You got what you wanted and stepped on me to get it." I told Secretary Buddy I was not on his team, and I would treat his administration as I did Rico. I would expose the corrupt actions of this department until the day I am gone, but he did not say much. I also told him he violated the civil service rules as they pertain to my grievance, and I planned to appeal his decision to civil service.

One month later, civil service accepted my appeal, and the entire rating was expunged from the record. So the warrior in me was resurrected, and the fight was on.

Harassment and Sick Leave

My checks began to get lost in the mail. My uniform cleaning allowance was denied. Subterfuge was the order of the day. I was ordered to take sick leave, which I appealed to civil service, and the department lost. My defense was that none of my supervisors, especially Lieutenant Colonel Silver Tongue, had a medical degree. Only a medical doctor could place me on sick leave. The harassment went on and on.

During my four-month hiatus on sick leave, I began compiling notes on how much overtime I had to work over the years. I gave the state thousands of hours dedicated toward my job. During my first two years, I worked seven days a week. I did not take any annual leave for the first twelve years. As already noted I went twenty-one years without taking any sick leave. The seven-days-a-week routine was too much to take; therefore, I decided I wouldn't be around much longer, so in 1996, I filed a federal lawsuit against the state for violating the Fair Labor Standards Act.

Immediately, the working of overtime without pay stopped. This action sent a shockwave throughout the state. The practice of intimidating agents to give time was in jeopardy. The state did not know how to react. They were losing their precious control.

STATE OF LOUISIANA
DEPARTMENT OF CIVIL SERVICE
P. O. BOX 94111, CAPITOL STATION BATON ROUGE, LA 70804-9111

Allen H. Reynolds
Director

Appeals Division
(225) 342-8070
Fax. (225) 342-8058
TDD 1-800-846-5277
http://www.dscs.state.la.us

ROY CHAUVIN

v.

DEPARTMENT OF WILDLIFE &
FISHERIES

State of Louisiana
Civil Service Commission
Docket No. 14455

Date: 8/13/01; Mailed. August 13, 2001
____ Fax'd _____

Notice to Agency of Possible Defects in Action

To: Department of Wildlife & Fisheries
Office of the General Counsel
Post Office Box 98000
Baton Rouge, Louisiana 70898-9000

I have reviewed the record in this appeal. The agency's action appears defective because:

_X__ The agency has no authority to place an employee on forced sick leave.

Therefore, you are hereby ordered to show cause, in writing, within 15 calendar days from the date at the top of this notice why I should not summarily grant this appeal due to the defect(s) noticed above.

Bernice R. Pellegrin
Civil Service Commission Referee

cc: Mr. Roy Chauvin, Jr.
Mr. James Jenkins, Jr.
Pending cases
Tickler
File

AP:BRP:kdw

** NOTE: We accept all filings by fax -- 225/342-8058 and **
by e-mail -- www.dscsappeals@dscs.state.la.us

AN EQUAL OPPORTUNITY EMPLOYER

The Transfer

The department finally mustered up enough guts to take a drastic step in their attempt to rid them of a problem. On August 28, 1996, I was transferred to the statewide oyster task force. The purpose was to push me into an obscure position separated from the entire enforcement division. I had become the Pied Piper when it came to overtime. Employees from throughout the state in the LDWF sought my advice on such a move. Colonel Cook sugarcoated the move saying I would be in charge, make my own schedule, not work overtime, take leave, and finally, be under the supervision of Major Smoozer. Major Smoozer had the reputation of sticking a knife in your back and making you enjoy it. I was told to set up my office with the biologists whom some of which I had investigated. Needless to say, I was not greeted with open arms.

No matter what happened to me, I would always turn a bad situation into something workable. I still had the zeal to protect wildlife. Our jurisdiction as the Oyster Strike Force did not limit our activities strictly to oysters. There were thousands and thousands of acres of oysters leased from the state, which had to be safeguarded from theft. This statewide position opened up a new world of work. Periodically, there were closed areas of oyster harvesting due to pollution. Polluted oysters were a priority due to the fact that people with weak immune systems were at risk of serious illnesses and even death. Thus, the current written warning issued at all outlets who sell raw oysters.

Refrigeration of Oysters

The handling of oysters was a critical part of our job. The Louisiana Department of Health had immediate oversight. The Food and Drug Administration monitored the Louisiana Board of Health. As my roots set in the Oyster Strike Force, I targeted several areas of abuse that needed attention.

In order to track illnesses, every sack of oysters had to be tagged with the date of harvest, the place of harvest, and the harvester's name and license number. During the months of July, August, and September, we experience extremely hot days in the South; therefore, priority was proper refrigeration. The oysters were to be stored at ambient air temperatures of forty-five degrees with one degree of temperature higher the bacterial growth rate increases dramatically. We would set up operations at truck stops to check the temperatures of the trucks carrying oysters. This move was not popular at all. The typical pressure was placed on me at the scene. The rue was the same. The owner of the oysters would complain, followed by the politician calling, then followed by my department.

The cases varied from inadequate refrigeration to no refrigeration at all. We recorded temperatures in unrefrigerated trucks up to one hundred degrees Fahrenheit.

After numerous raids and seizures, it was decided by the oyster industry to call me on the carpet. The meeting consisted of fishermen, politicians, the board of health, and Department of Wildlife and Fisheries. I was accompanied by Major Smoozer, who stated I could not talk at the meeting of over one hundred people. Many took turns shooting my tactics down. One state representative, who was very vocal and politically motivated, was very critical of me personally. I was muzzled and didn't like it. Major Smoozer said nothing to defend me, or the Oyster Strike Force.

There was major discussion at this meeting to raise the legal temperature of oyster storage containers to fifty degrees, up from forty-five degrees. The Louisiana Board of Health had the renegade authority to do so. After collapsing under pressure, the Board of Health decided to raise the ambient air temperature to fifty degrees. Fishermen applauded the move as well as dealers. Many shouted, "Take that, Chauvin!" as they left the meeting laughing.

Approximately one month after the fifty-degree rule went into effect, I received a call from the Food and Drug Administration stating that a forty-five-year-old Florida woman, in good health, had died after eating raw oysters from Louisiana. Adverse publicity was a death blow to the sensitive industry. Often, expansive closures would go into effect until the problem could be narrowed down through an investigation.

Immediately, the Board of Health began to scramble. The Food and Drug Administration called out the Board of Health for changing the temperature to fifty degrees. The Board of Health, therefore, changed the rule back to forty-five degrees and asked for my help in diffusing the situation. I lashed out at the industry, politicians, Board of Health, and the federal Food and Drug Administration for allowing someone to die during their political games. The state could not muzzle me anymore. Everyone hung their heads in shame and fear.

Norwalk Virus

During the same time, a huge outbreak of Norwalk virus affecting some six hundred people in the Southeastern United States was attributed to oysters from Louisiana. Immediately, the entire east side of the Mississippi River was closed to harvesting oysters. This turned out to be a great monetary blow to the state. The adverse publicity affected the entire state. People were leery of eating raw oysters. The Center for Disease Control of Atlanta, Georgia, sent a team of scientists to investigate the cause of the outbreak. The technical aspect of the case came down to researching tags on oyster sacks and records of shipments of oysters.

It was determined that the incident may have been caused by an extremely low tide, no water movement, and the illness of crew members aboard a vessel. The findings were such that the crew possibly had the illness supporting the virus, which caused diarrhea and vomiting.

The crew released the virus overboard and continued to harvest oysters in the same area. Billions of viral particles, according to the Center for Disease Control, were released into the water. Oysters are a filter, taking in water to eat. However, some particles in the water are retained. Half-shell oysters are famous throughout the country. The oysters have to be kept alive during the process just prior to consumption. Any breakdown in the process could render disastrous effects.

CHAPTER 25

Beginning of the End

During my tenure in the Oyster Strike Force, I met with other supervisors throughout the state to establish a base of cooperation. I reached out to the captain of Region 5 who said his number-one problem with oysters was a dealer in Cameron, Louisiana. The captain said Oyster Man had total control of Cameron Parish, and no one could do anything with him. Oyster fishing in Cameron was a very regulated fishery. One could only take ten sacks per day. There was also a large area closed due to pollution.

Cameron is a small remote town on the Gulf of Mexico, somewhat like Grand Isle. Cameron Parish had a total population of approximately six thousand residents who all knew each other. I was told by the local agents there was a total lack of cooperation with the sheriff and the judge when it came to dealing with Oyster Man. Of course, this intrigued and challenged me.

In November of 1996, I decided to go to Cameron to meet Oyster Man. I took all three members of the Oyster Strike Force with me. We showed up at a camper trailer, which was the business place of Oyster Man. Here was this sixty-year-old man working oysters. I introduced myself and told Oyster Man we were there to make a routine inspection of licenses, tags, and records of purchases and sales. Oyster Man stated that his daughter, Oyster Lady, had the records at her house. We later met with Oyster Lady who stated she had the records, but they were very messy, and she asked if I would give her time to produce a computer-generated copy of the records. I agreed, and we did not issue any citations. Cameron was two hundred miles from my house, so the trip was not like going next door. It was very time-consuming. Since the Oyster Man operation had been booked several times before by the local agents, a resentment had developed between agents and Oyster Man. The local agents had given up on dealing with Oyster Man citing no convictions.

Approximately two months had passed, so on January 27, 1997, I decided to go back to Cameron to pick up records that Oyster Lady had promised. On this day, our reception was not as welcome as our November 1996 visit. We met Oyster Man at his business place, and I asked for the records. Oyster Man just walked around, totally ignoring me. I pressed harder, still trying to maintain a low-key attitude. Oyster Man continued to ignore me. On the third occasion that Oyster Man began to walk away, I explained the consequences of his noncompliance. He continued to ignore me. I told Oyster Man I would give him one more chance, or he would be arrested for numerous wildlife violations. Again, he ignored me. Oyster Man said, "I don't have any records, and I am not going to give you any records." I instructed the agents to arrest him. Oyster Man resisted as the agent attempted to place the handcuffs on him. The agent was following procedure by handcuffing an uncooperative subject behind his back. Oyster Man said the cuffs were hurting. I asked Oyster Man if he would get in the car if I placed the cuffs in the front. Oyster Man said yes, and he got into my car.

It was getting dark, and Oyster Man had an entourage of family waiting at the entrance of the jail. We walked into the lockup area at the sheriff's office only to be confronted with a cold group of silent deputies. I told the jailer we were there to lock up Oyster Man for wildlife violations. The jailer and deputies walked off. I had never been in a place like this with such total lack of cooperation. The deputies talked to Oyster Man trivializing our investigation.

Oyster Man ordered one of the deputies to take off the handcuffs. Oyster Man then instructed another deputy to get him something to drink as he roamed outside the detention area. The crowd grew larger outside the jail. I confronted the jailer asking what they were going to do. The jailer sarcastically told me they would not lock up Oyster Man, and the jailer walked away. At this time, I turned to the agents and told them we weren't accomplishing anything. I felt it was best to leave the situation before it got worse.

As we left the jail, Oyster Lady produced some records for October through December 1996. About one week later, she produced the January 1997 books.

It was obvious that there was no law enforcement at all in Cameron Parish. I had entered into their sacred grounds where outsiders were not welcomed. The local agents were intimidated by these tactics and had no respect from Oyster Man. Well, this was a classic case of corruption and collusion by local law enforcement. I decided to take on the challenge, which distracted me from many other crises for the next four years.

Four-Year-Long Federal Grand Jury

I had to come up with a different approach. I met with federal agent and friend, Bill Ferguson, from Lake Charles. Bill said he had heard that I had been ran out of Cameron. I asked Bill if he would help me develop a case on Oyster Man since the oysters were going out of the state and presented a public health risk. The federal government's jurisdiction was covered under the Lacey Act, which simply stated any wildlife taken in violation of state law and transported across state lines is a federal violation of the Lacey Act.

Bill and I met with Assistant United States Attorney JM and CD to discuss a strategy. The violation occurred in the Western District of Louisiana, which had federal jurisdiction. I explained the seriousness of the violations as they pertained to public safety. Joining us in the initial meeting was an FBI agent.

The FBI agent asked if we were going to Cameron. The agent said, "Good luck. You won't get any cooperation." The agent said the last witness they looked for in Cameron was found dead in a camp a couple of weeks after their search.

The Assistant US attorney, JM, decided that it was fruitless to confront Oyster Man anymore. JM would convene a federal grand jury and subpoenas for records and other information would be sought.

I met with Agent Ferguson in Cameron shortly thereafter to begin interviewing fishermen. Nearly everyone in town fished for Oyster Man. The impact of asking questions on behalf of a federal grand jury did have its advantages. However, most witnesses hid from us and were very hard to track down.

One night after interviews, I was escorted out of town by deputies. The deputies followed me all the way to Lafayette, Louisiana, approximately one hundred miles from their jurisdiction. This was not new to me.

On another run to Cameron to issue federal grand jury subpoenas, Bill and I were in a line of cars in his unmarked vehicle when a Cameron deputy singled us out of the line, put his flashing lights on, and stopped Bill. Bill knew the deputy and questioned his intentions. Bill said, "My cruise control was set on fifty-five, the speed limit." The deputy said he was speeding. Bill became very upset, and the deputy called for backup, which usually ends in an arrest. I told Bill they were going to arrest him. Now the other Cameron Parish deputies showed up. Bill told the two deputies he knew what was going on and informed the deputies that we were acting upon the orders of the United States attorney in Lafayette. "We are here to issue federal grand jury subpoenas, and you are currently obstructing justice and the grand jury process." The deputies left immediately. Well, everyone in Cameron scrambled. They knew we were coming.

Bill said he knew one honest deputy in Cameron that he could trust. We met with the deputy who stated we had things buzzing in Cameron. The deputy assisted us in locating only a few witnesses.

As part of the investigation, we began to decipher Oyster Lady's original books presented on January 29, 1997. The records were a mess as Oyster Lady had said. We were able to determine over $400,000 went through Oyster Man's company in less than three months. Shipments of oysters went to Alabama, Florida, North Carolina, and Virginia. The records also gave us a few numbers and names to start our investigation. Immediately, we began to find inconsistencies and noted there were numerous violations in the first set of books.

Agent Ferguson and I began the lengthy process of finding and interviewing fishermen, some of which lived out of the state. After months of interviewing the fishermen and dealers listed on the first set of records, Oyster Lady in May of 1997 produced a second set of books in an effort to correct numerous false entries in the first set of records received on January 29, 1997. This delayed the investigation and presented a whole new list of inconsistencies.

The investigation was so technical that in one entry, there was an individual who allegedly allowed someone to use his boat to fish. The registration on the boat had expired months before, but a new registration was applied for by the boat owner according to Louisiana Department of Wildlife and Fisheries official records. It was discovered the application for the boat registration was applied for on a specific date; however, the owner of the boat had died long before the application was submitted. We had to get another agent in another state to research the death records where the owner had died. The certificate of death of the owner showed that the owner did not apply for the boat registration due to the fact that he was dead. This was just one of the exhibits in this complicated trial.

During the four-year-long federal grand jury investigation, we compiled a list of eighty-plus witnesses, all of whom were interviewed and produced over three thousand exhibits of evidence to be presented at trial.

Another aspect of this complicated case were the entries of several fishermen who were listed as fishing on certain days. It was discovered through interviews with company officials, and verified by records, these men could not have fish on those days. Their work records listed them working at their offshore oil field jobs at the same time. This act was done to circumvent the ten sacks for fishermen, per day regulation.

There were admissions by some fishermen that, during days of bad weather, they fished in the closed/polluted areas and sold their catch to Oyster Man. Since the oysters were more plentiful in the closed area, some fishermen made multiple trips fishing and selling to Oyster Man.

After four years of investigation and federal grand jury proceedings, Oyster Man, Oyster Lady, and the company were indicted by the grand jury on fifteen felony counts. Shortly thereafter, the trial was scheduled before Federal District Judge T in Lake Charles. At the ten-day jury trial, the suspects were found guilty on all counts except count thirteen.

Immediately, the defense counsel filed a lengthy appeal motion for judgment of acquittal and a motion for a new trial. Both motions were denied on November 27, 2000, and the convictions were upheld.

The Race Card

In a very strange turn of events after the trial and appeal, I was summoned before the trial judge in Lake Charles accompanied by Assistant US Attorney JM. I was informed that the defense attorney allegedly had ties to Governor Rico. Attending the "whatever it was" in Judge T chambers was the defense attorney and the foreman of the ten-day jury trial. I did not have a clue what was happening, but Assistant US Attorney JM instructed me to answer questions and not volunteer anything.

The defense attorney started the meeting by stating that the foreman of the jury trial wanted to change his verdict. Strange but true. The defense attorney stated my actions throughout the case were racist. The attorneys stated that Oyster Man was black. Further stating that I had discriminated against Oyster Man's whole family and him due to his race.

The judge asked the foreman why hadn't he brought this up before the trial. The foreman had no valid answer. The judge also told the foreman he had sat there for ten days, became foreman of the jury, and chose to find Oyster Man and his daughter guilty on fourteen out of fifteen counts.

"Is that not correct?" asked the judge.

The foreman said, "Yes, but I changed my mind."

The foreman seemed very unsure of himself and looked like he wanted out of the room.

My impression and thinking was someone got to the foreman, and for whatever reason, the foreman brought up these allegations in order to tamper with a verdict and system.

Upset, the judge further stated that the foreman heard testimony from me stating that I had violated procedure during handcuffing to accommodate Oyster Man. The judge said that gesture alone negated the discrimination claim. The judge continued to chastise the foreman and told the attorney the information was insufficient during the trial and at this meeting to remotely substantiate discrimination by me. The judge then, abruptly, dismissed everyone. Assistant US Attorney JM said this was just dirty tactics and grabbing at straws.

I felt the foreman should have been investigated for conspiracy but that would have taken more and more time. Assistant US Attorney JM said this was a first for him and cited that my reputation followed me around.

On January 25, 2001, Oyster Man was sentenced to thirty months in the US Bureau of Prisons. He was placed on supervised release after his prison term and was to perform 150 hours of community service during the first eighteen months of supervised release. He was placed on two years of probation and ordered to pay an assessment of $1,400.

Oyster Lady was sentenced to thirty-seven months in federal prison with two years of supervised probation upon release. She also had to perform 150 hours of community service and pay an assessment of $1,500 and a fine of $5,000.

The Seafood Company was also found guilty and ordered to pay an assessment of $5,600.

There is no good-time policy for prisoners in the federal system; therefore, one has to serve the full term.

I wondered if Oyster Man gave orders to jailers in the federal system to take his cuffs off and get him a drink of water. I think not.

To my understanding, this was the most extensive case in the history of the Louisiana Department of Wildlife and Fisheries enforcement division.

Last Contact

What a better way to bid the corrupt farewell. However, I feel that corruption continues to exist, and the Ricos are out there, but the passing of time soothes the soul. At least I tried. On October 5, 2001, I went on extended sick leave, never to return to the corrupt practices that were so often a part of my life as a wildlife agent in Louisiana.

Just prior to my leave, poetic justice was served when former Governor Rico was found guilty of seventeen counts of racketeering influenced and corrupt organization act (RICO). In January 2001, Governor Rico was sentenced to ten years in federal prison. Seeing an old man go to prison did not alleviate the pain and suffering I had to endure, but I refuse to go to my grave with any bitterness because that would be a victory for the corrupt.

My last contact with the Department of Wildlife and Fisheries was on the trial date of my Fair Labor Standards Act claim. My presence sent chills to all as I walked the halls of the courthouse greeting all with a smile of success. This was the face I had to present for twenty-seven years. The judge in the case state that my supervisors had committed numerous criminal violations during the discovery phase of the suit. In order to avoid another whack by me, the state settled a lawsuit for an undisclosed amount. A final victory in my wretched career.

C'est la vie.

Slave Of Convictions

The inner being is motivated
By the serenity of the Call of the wild.
As one gazes up at the soaring eagle
He equates his convictions to that of a child.

Simplicity is the ultimate dictator
In the role of the natural scheme of things.
For the birth of an unblemished fawn
Casts no doubt, in the unwritten message she brings.

Camouflaged for necessity,
From foe as well as beguiling friend;
For fear was not innately instilled
Until infanthood came to an abrupt end.

By day or night the ignoble predator
Invades the wilderness domain.
For the sake of unleaven sport, not hunger,
The defenseless creatures are indiscriminately slain.

Neither the darkest depths of the ocean
Nor the snowy peaks jutting to the sky---
None, offer any unattainable refuge,
For decaying carcasses lay visible to the concerned eye.

Baffled by the unnatural pressures
With nowhere to run or hide,
Watching their numbers being decimated
Instinct to live, though tourchered, they cried.

The unmitigated cry for help is heard,
Not by all, but only a select few.
These are called to preserve wildlife,
Spurred not only by economics, but dedication too.

Outnumbered by the obstacles to bear
Brings one to his knees in tormenting disgust.
Intermittantly digressing from human to beast
As the total confusion spawns distrust.

However soo strong the irristable urge
To succumb to the tactics of Man's bigoted game,
The twisted mind relieves the pressures
By the luring of the Call from which he came.

The inner being is motivated
By the serenity of the Call of the wild.
As he has lengthened the life of the fawn
The tears are broken, in part, by a smile.

To whom, by whom, for whom,
unknown

ABOUT THE AUTHOR

Roy Chauvin was born March 11, 1950, in a small town of South Louisiana called Houma. He attended private Catholic schools where he excelled in academics and sports, earning him a scholarship in baseball to Nicholl's State University, where he graduated with honors (summa cum laude) in 1972. He then entered Loyola School of Law but decided he did not want to be a lawyer. The prominent oil industry would not employ him, citing he was overeducated. Therefore, he sought a job of security and outdoors, which resulted in becoming a wildlife agent for the State of Louisiana on June 10, 1974.

His family life began at four years old when his neighbor Sally Benoit told Roy's mom she would marry Roy someday. On August 8, 1970, Roy and Sally were married. Due to a very serious illness, Roy and Sally had no biological children. They were thirty-two years old when on June 16, 1982, they began the heartbreaking process of fostering children. Going from childless to five little special-needs boys in six months, the Chauvin's began a life-altering adventure, which resulted in years of service, fostering twenty-five long-term children. They adopted five children, still fostering a thirty-six-year-old autistic child and raising a grandchild abandoned by their adopted daughter. The child was eighteen months old and today is seventeen.

Sally and Roy have been married for fifty years due to a strong love they have for one another. Both reside in the Cajun town of Houma, Louisiana.

CPSIA information can be obtained
at www.ICGtesting.com
Printed in the USA
BVHW070727101121
621186BV00002B/125